AF374809

DANIEL RUCZKO

QUIT HATING ON SATAN!

A collection of horror images featuring the devil, inspired by the look of comic books from the 80s.

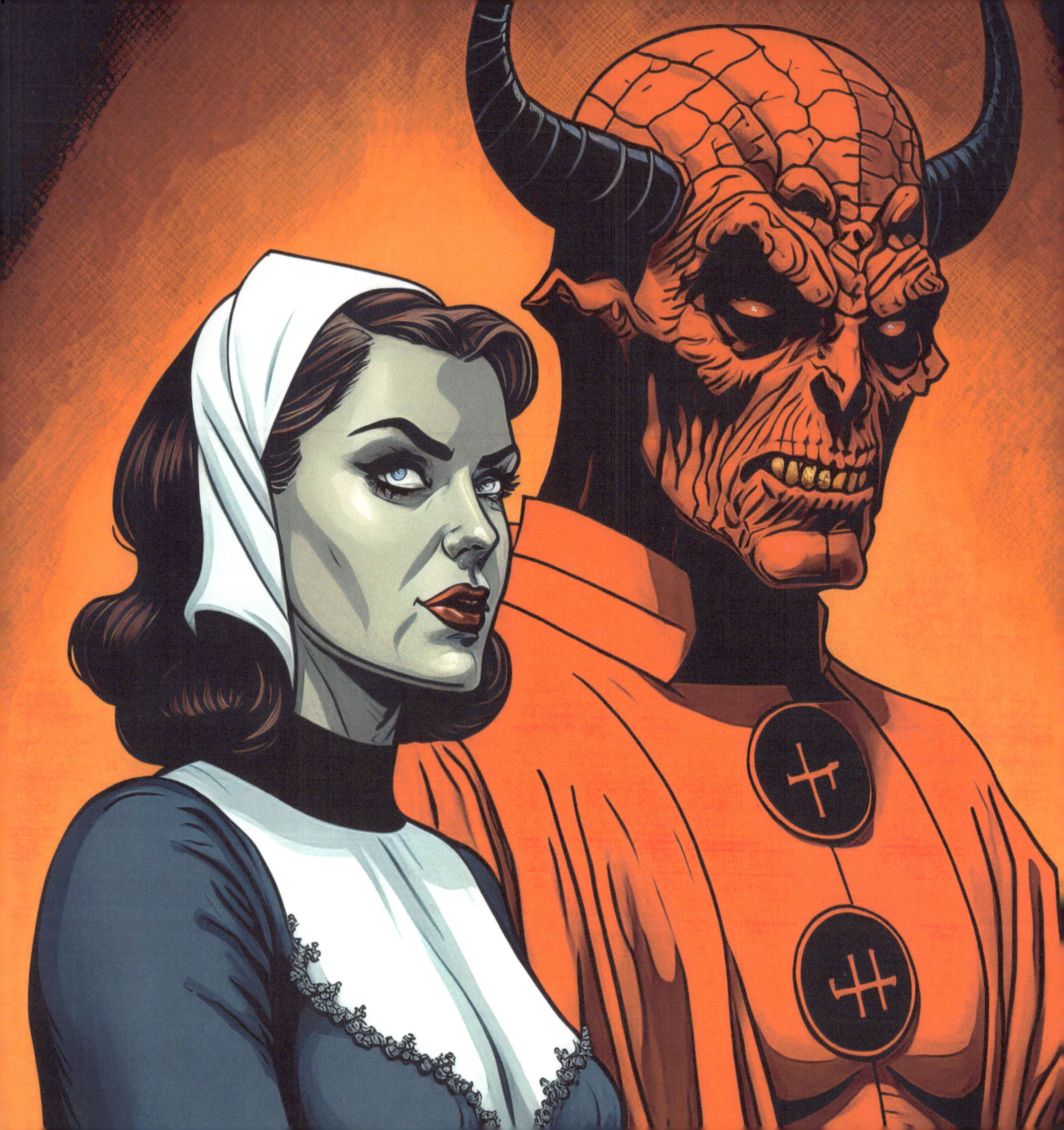

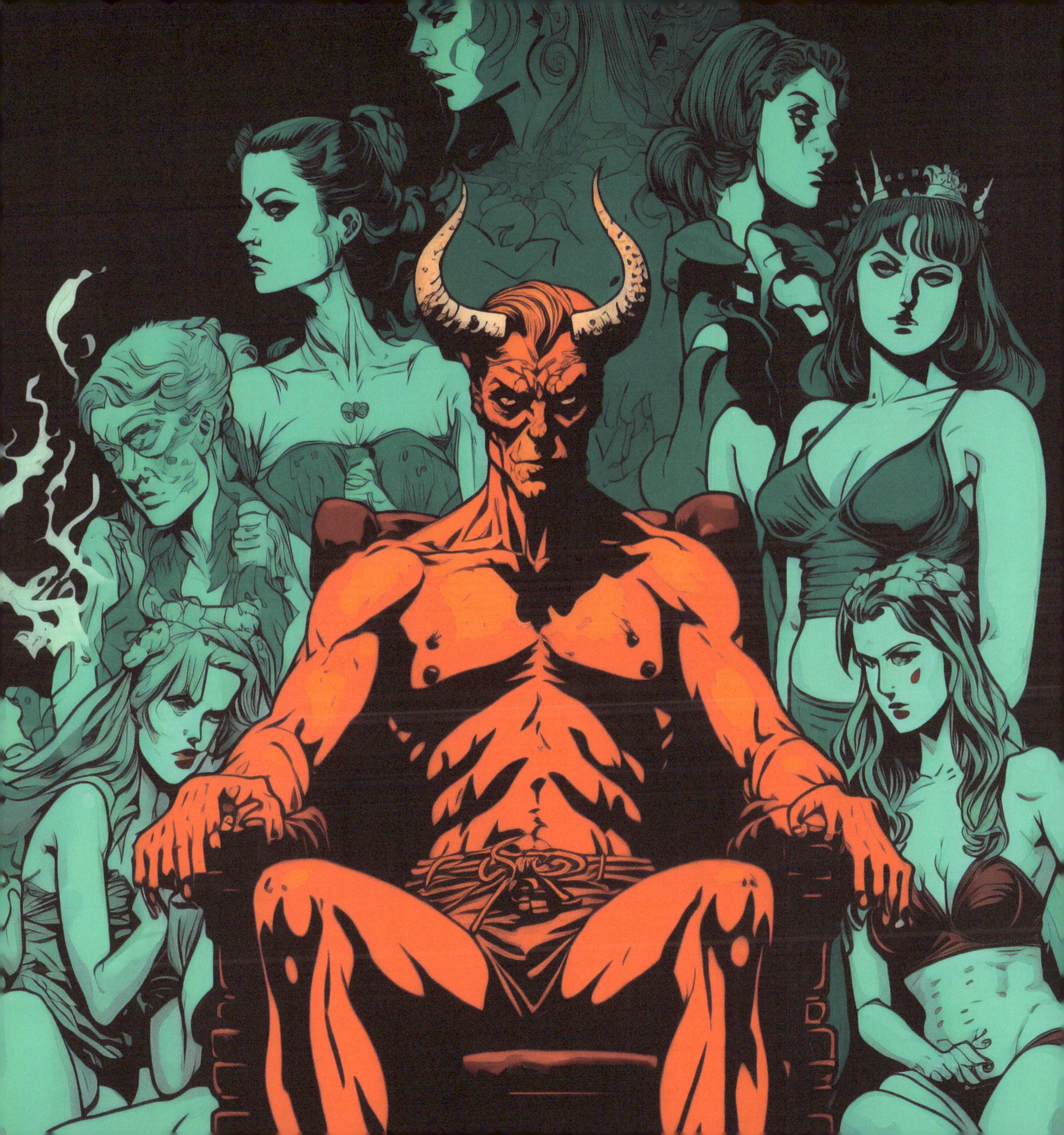

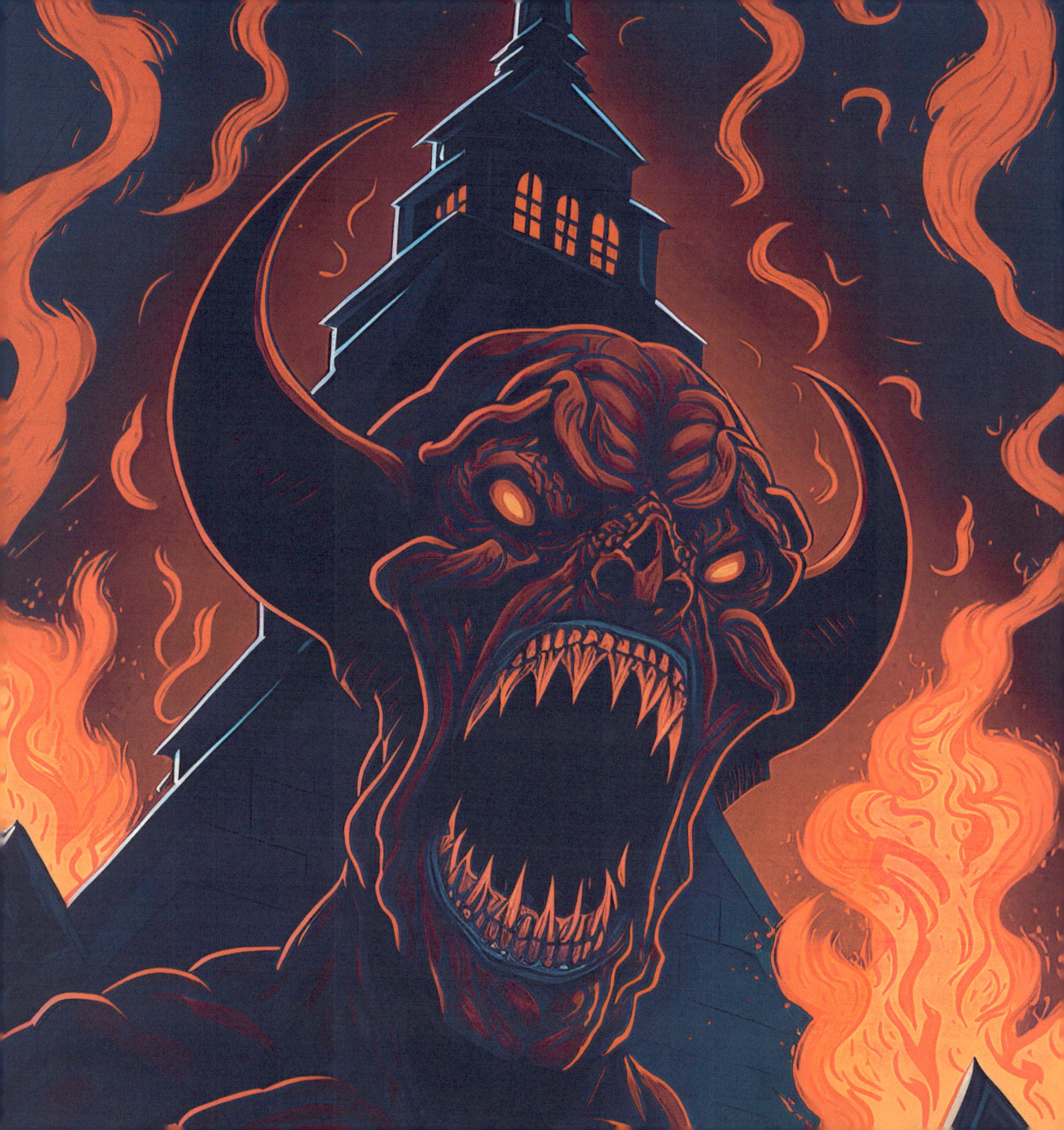

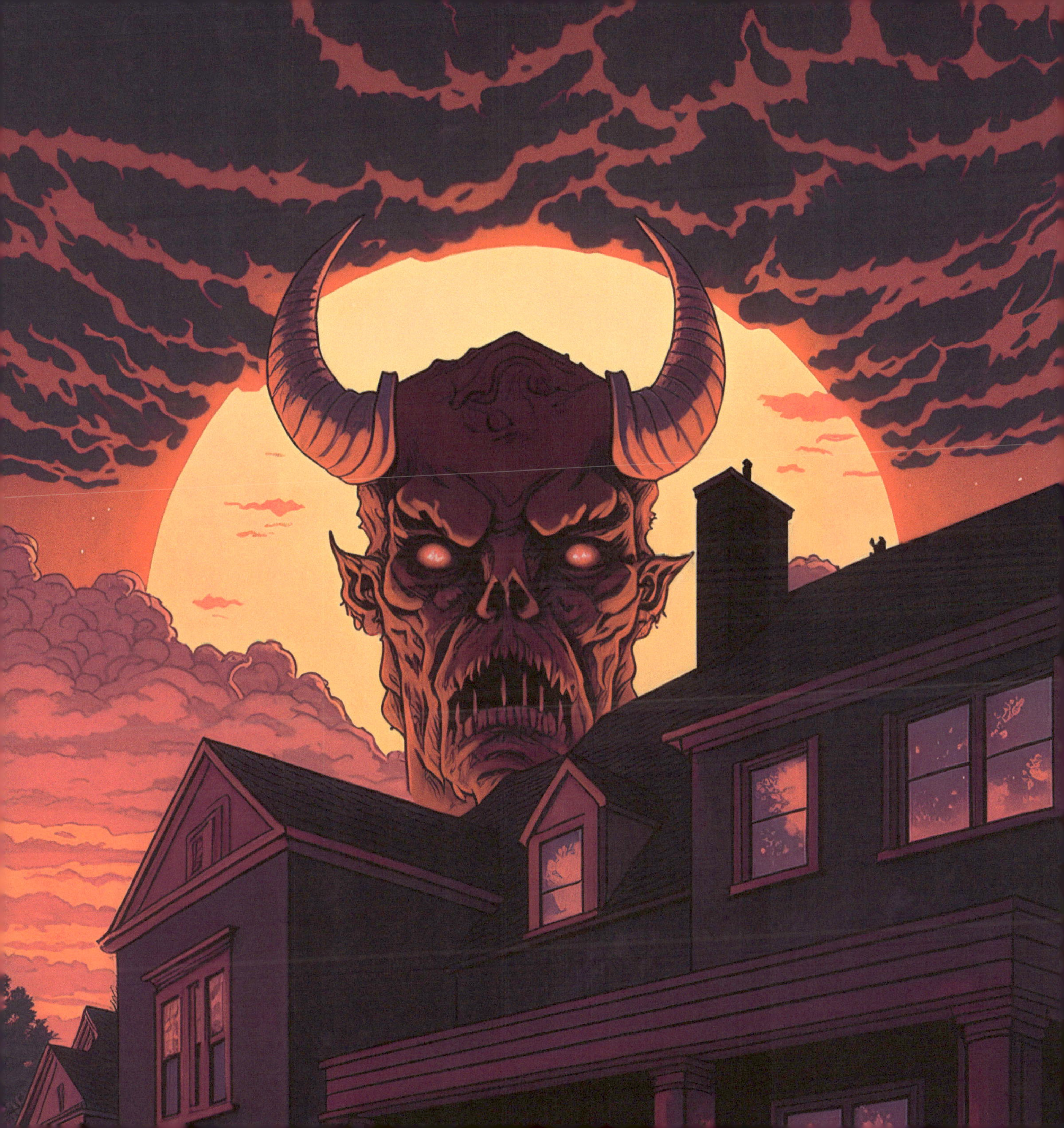

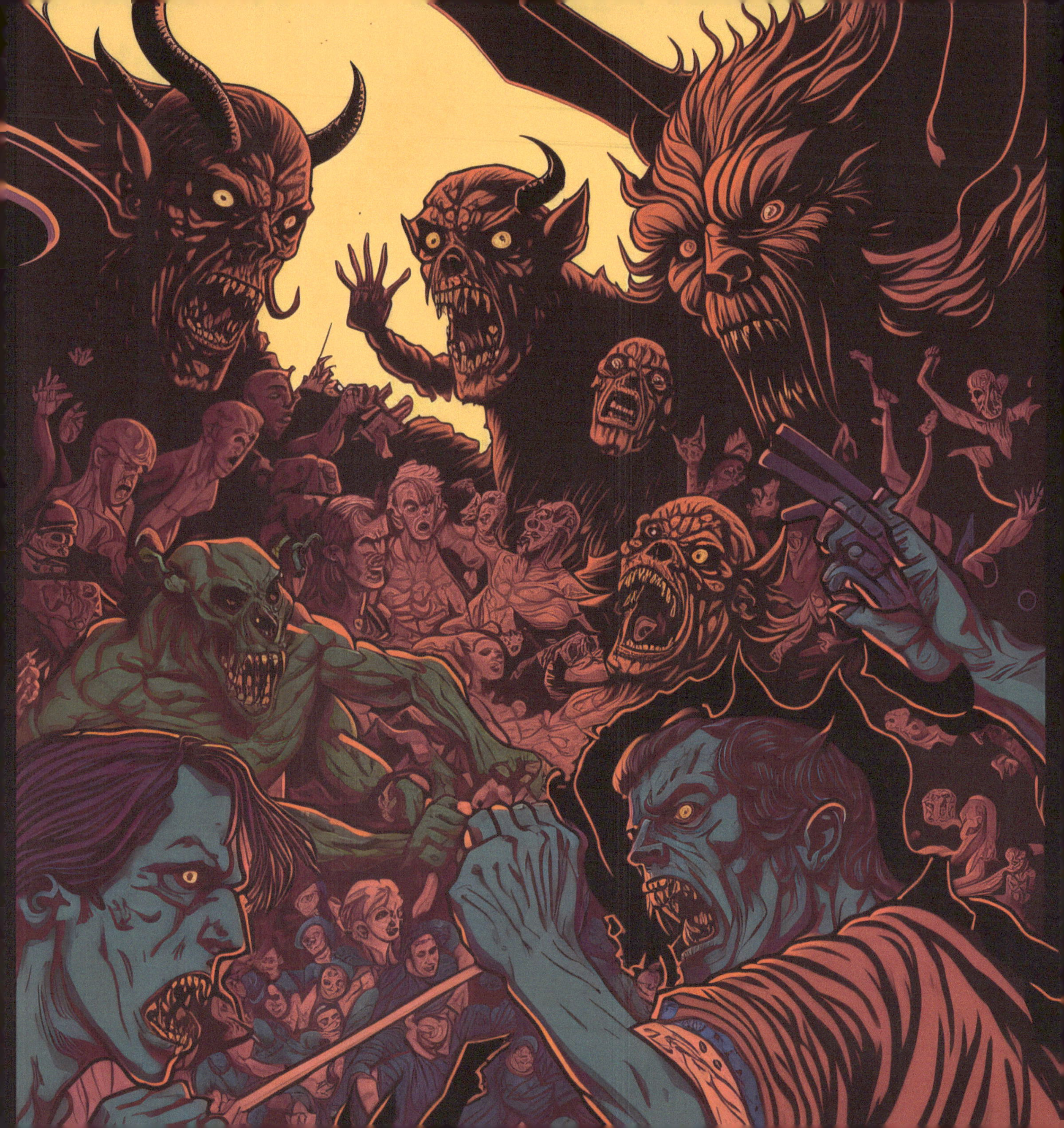

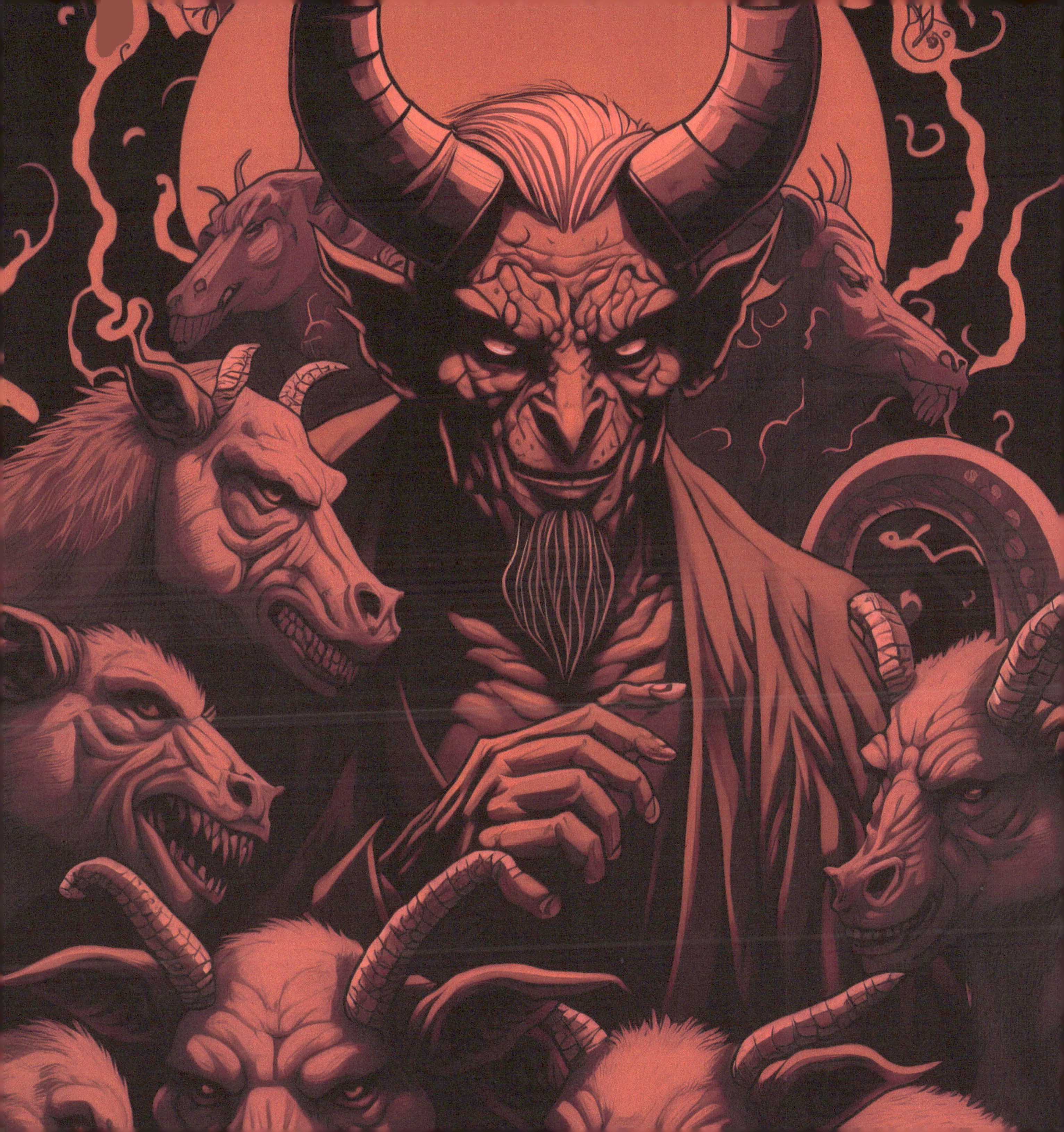

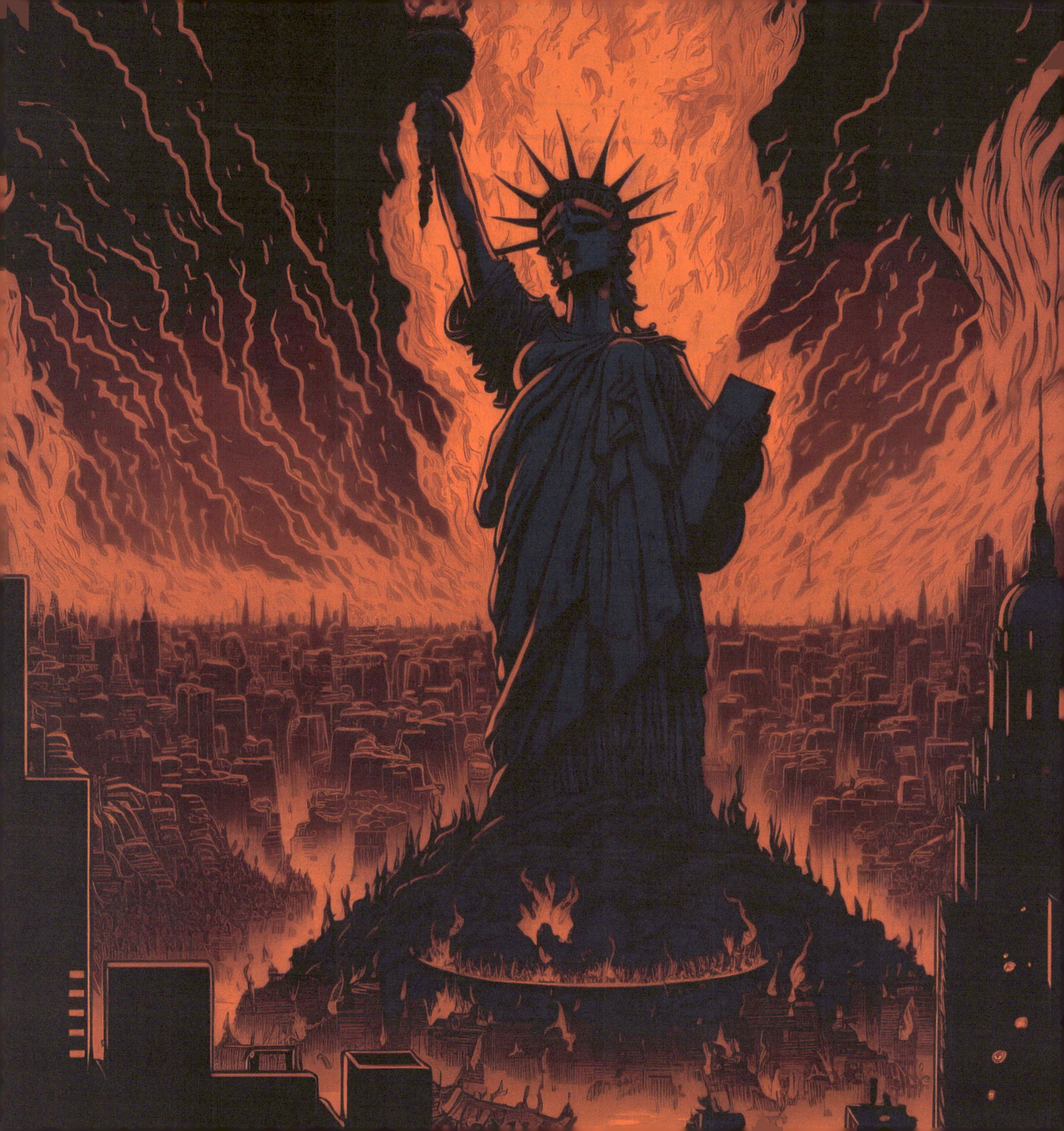

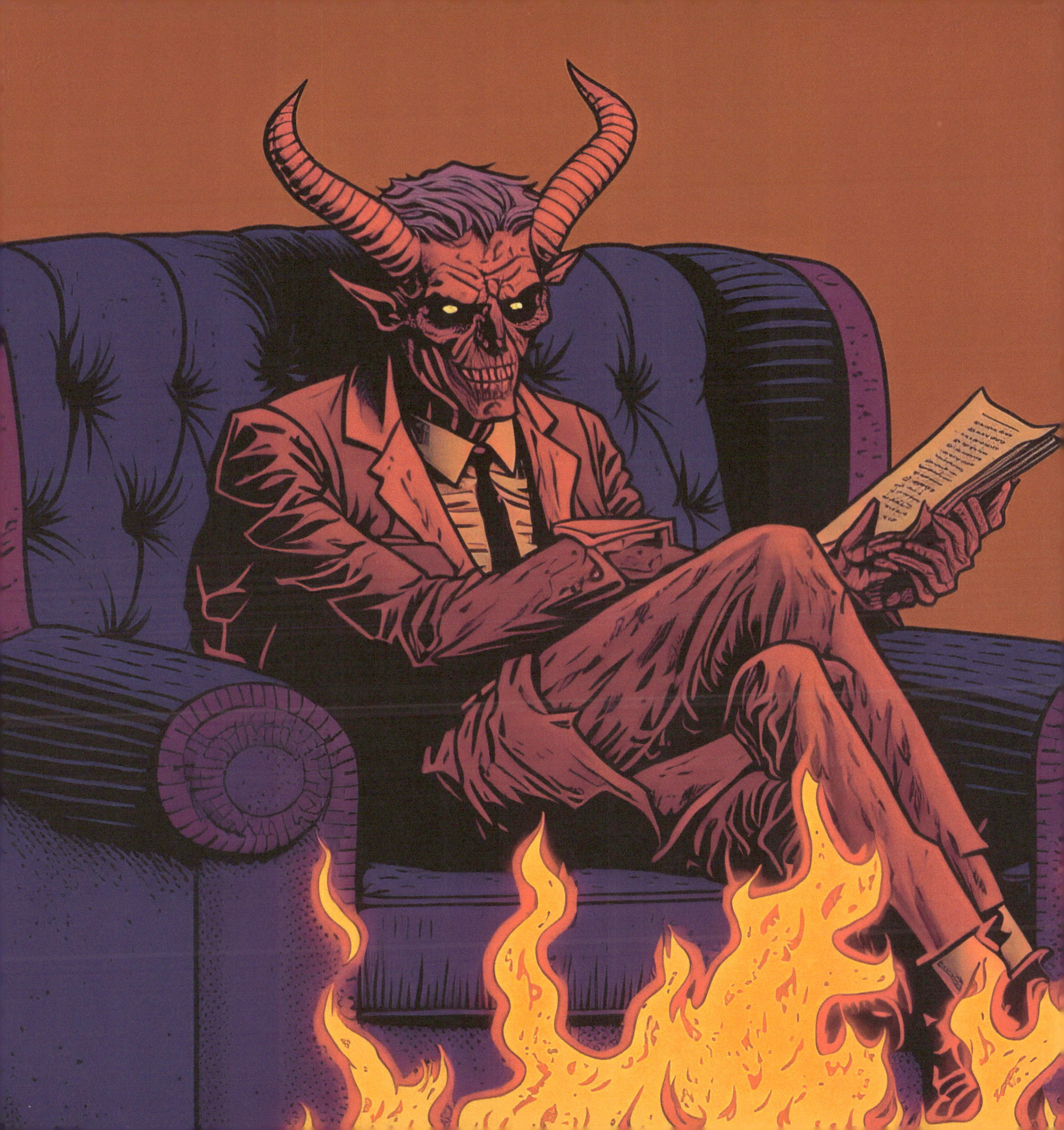

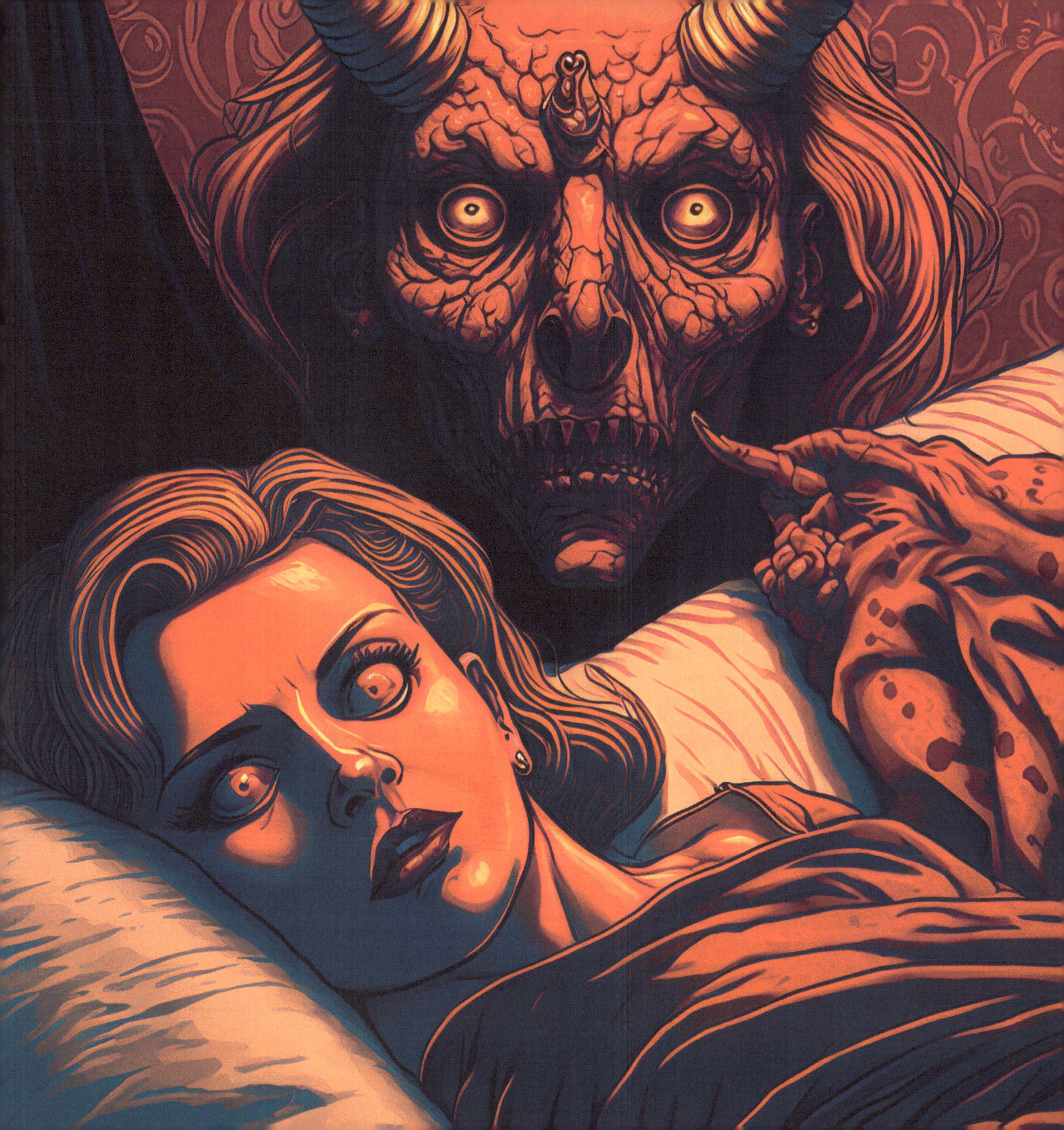

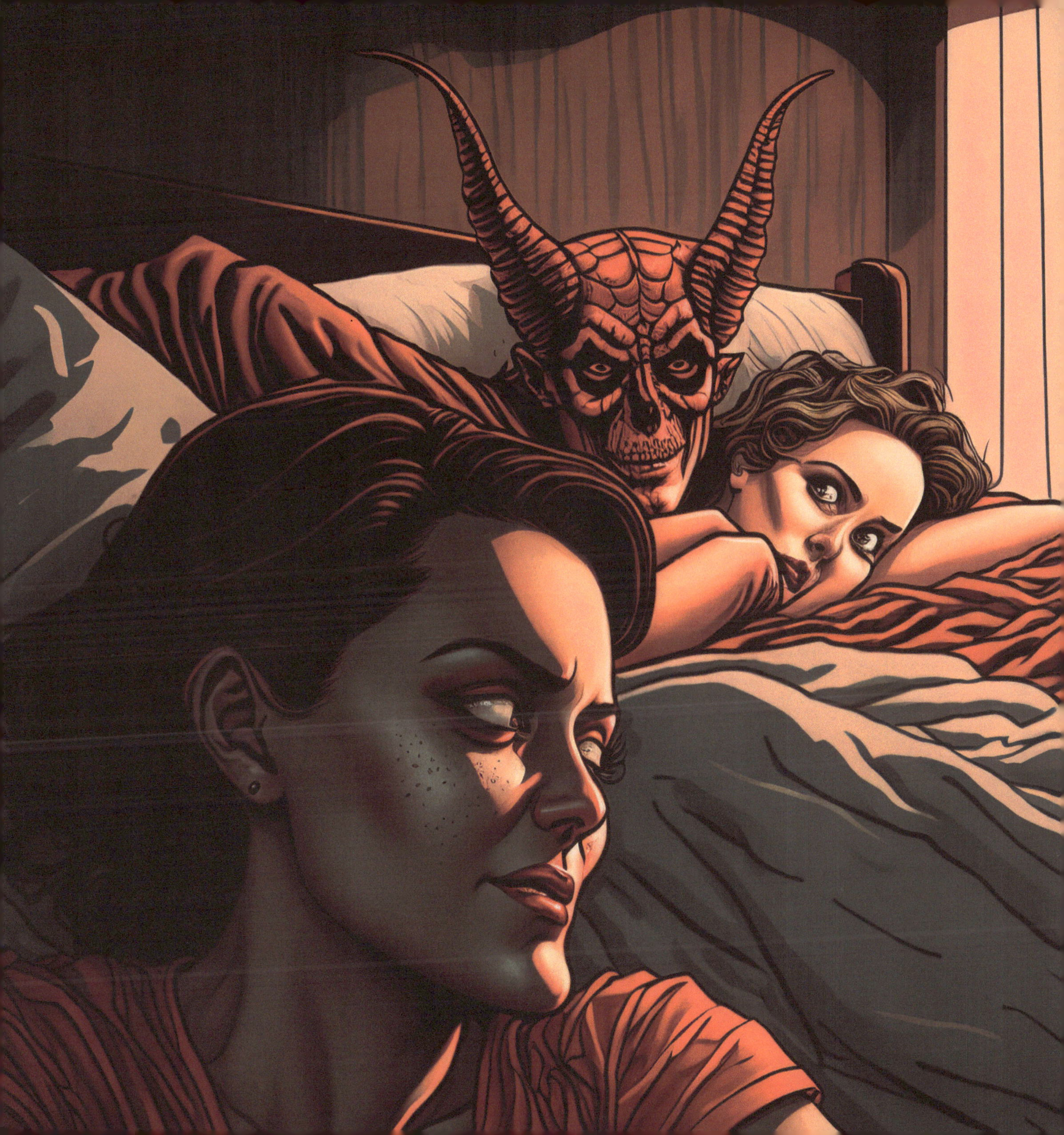

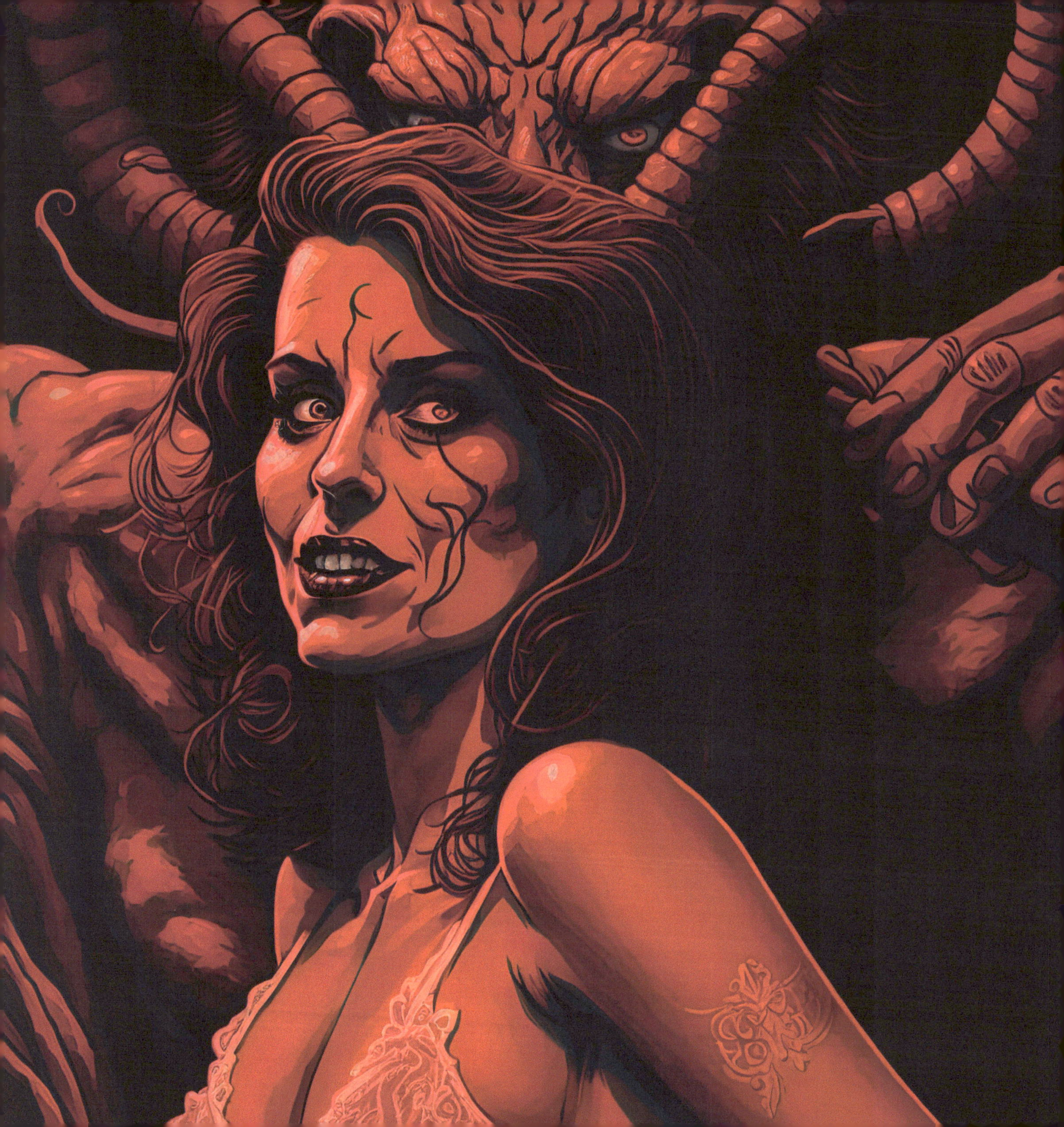

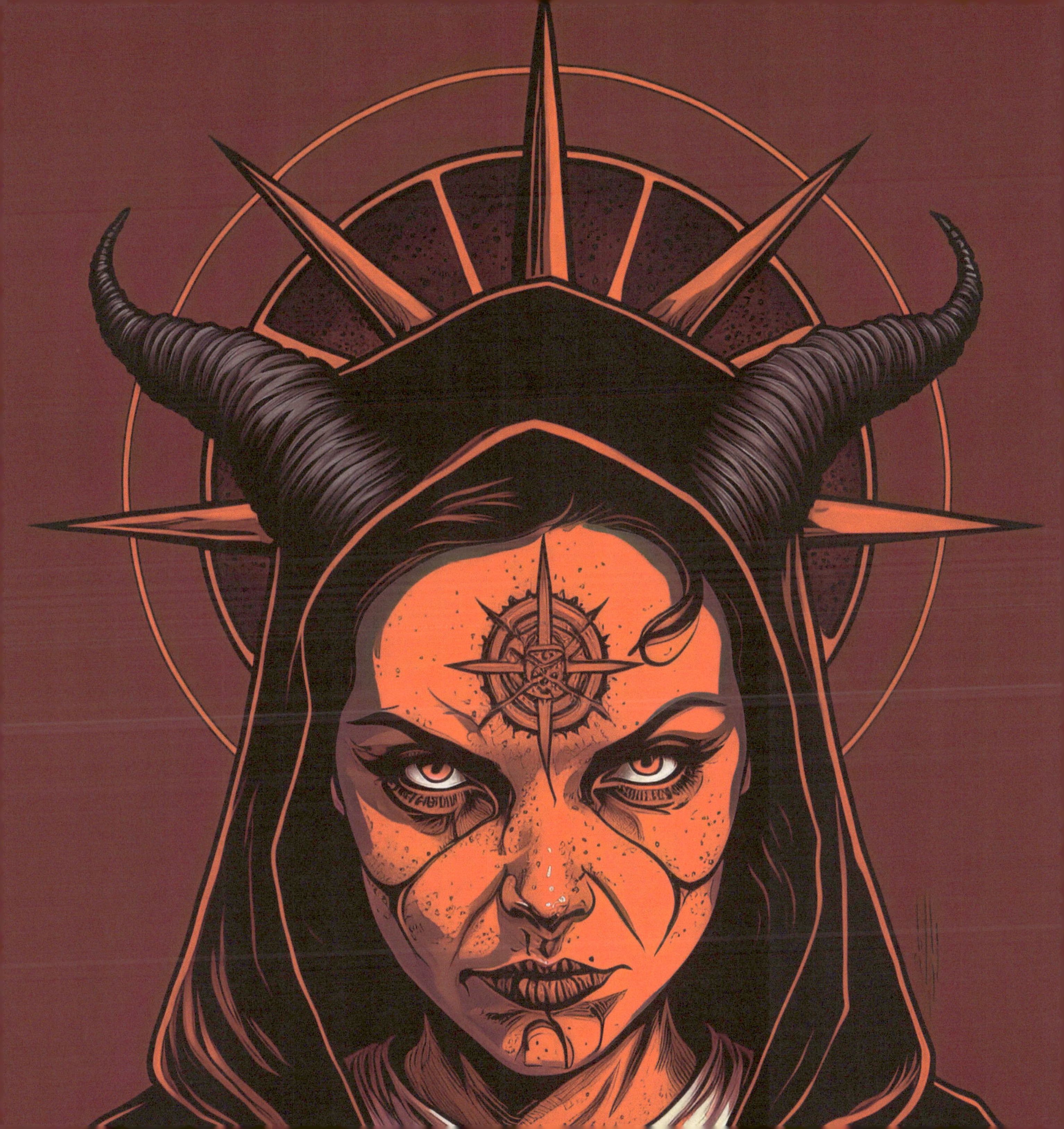

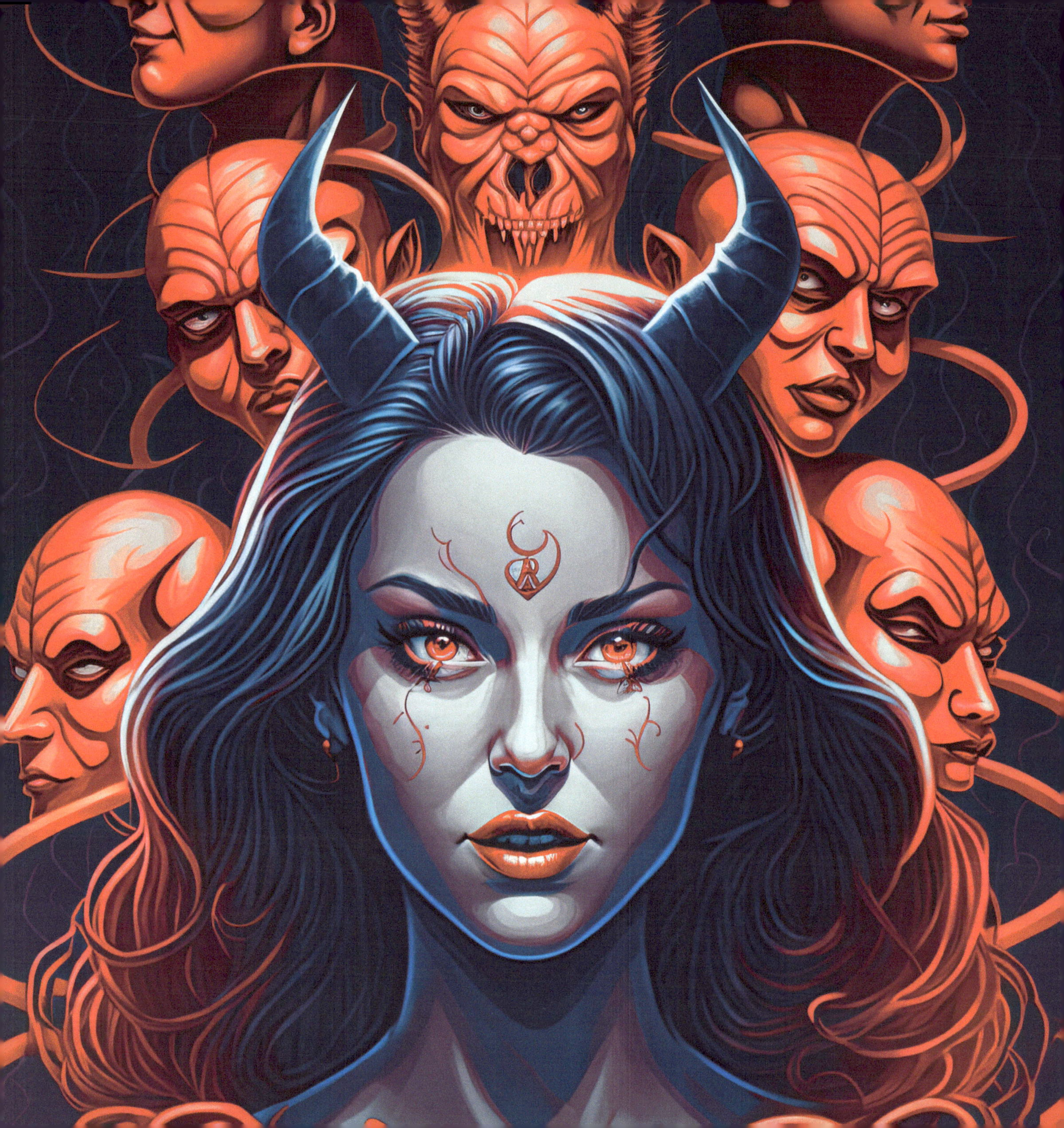

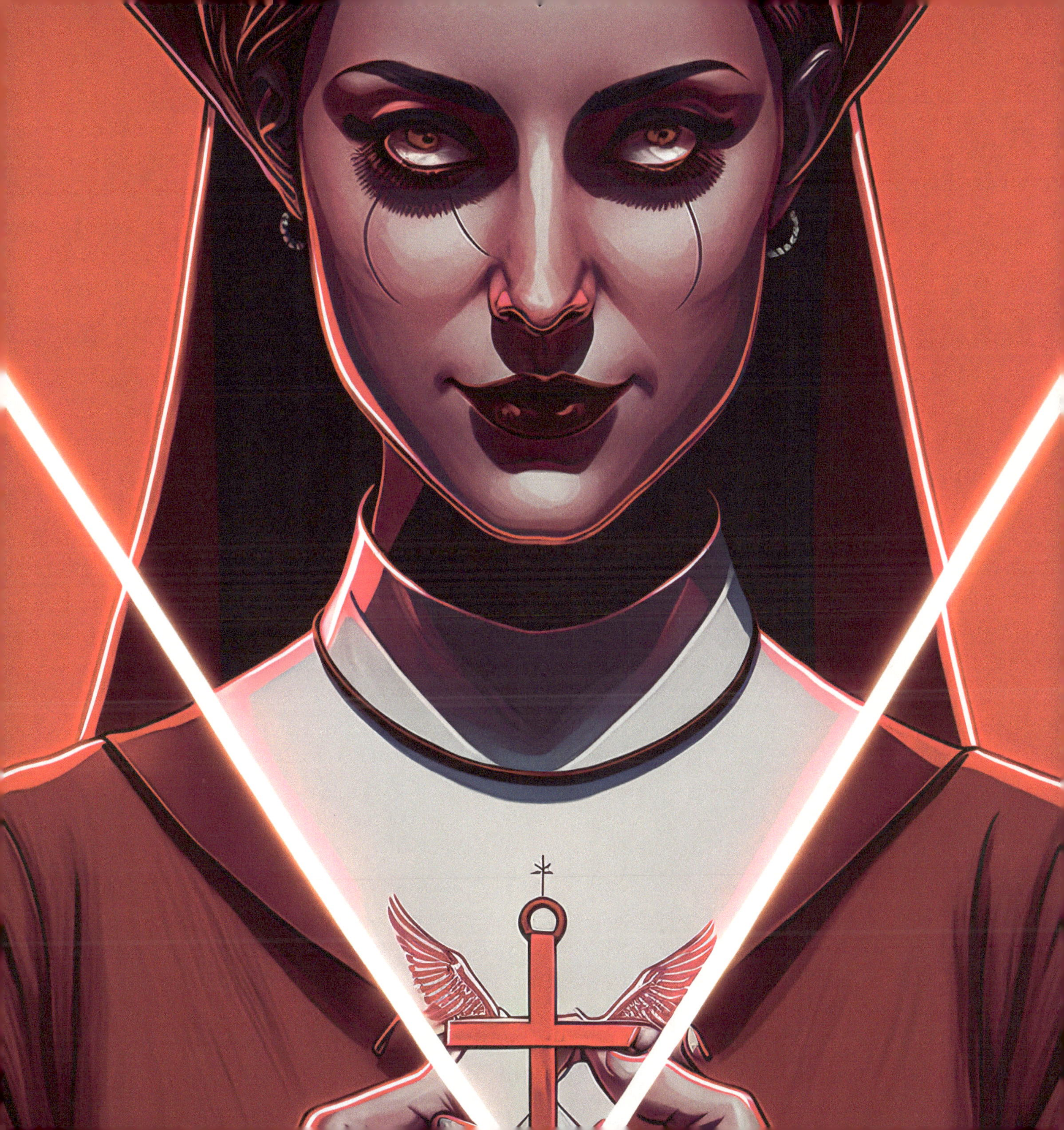

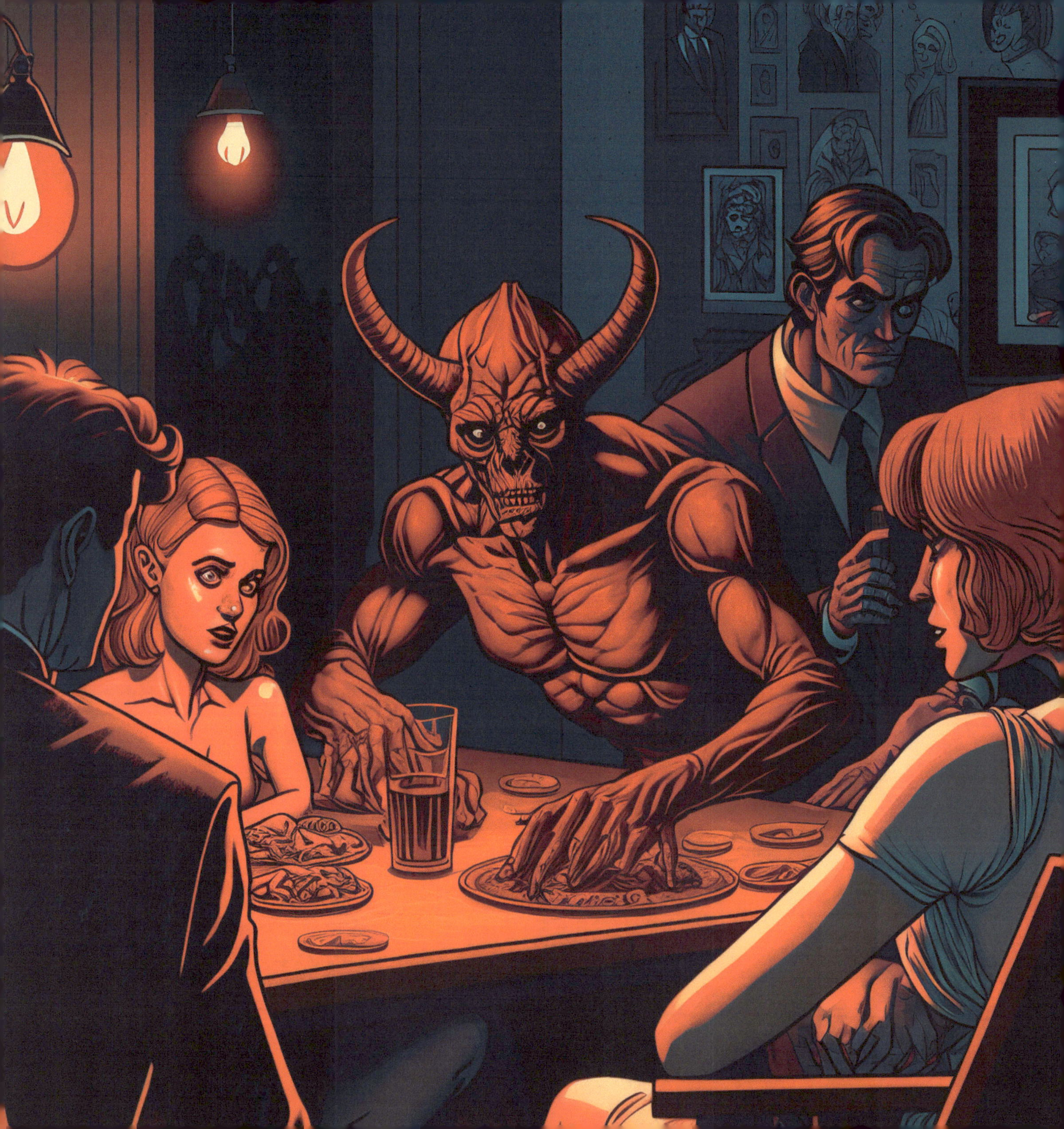

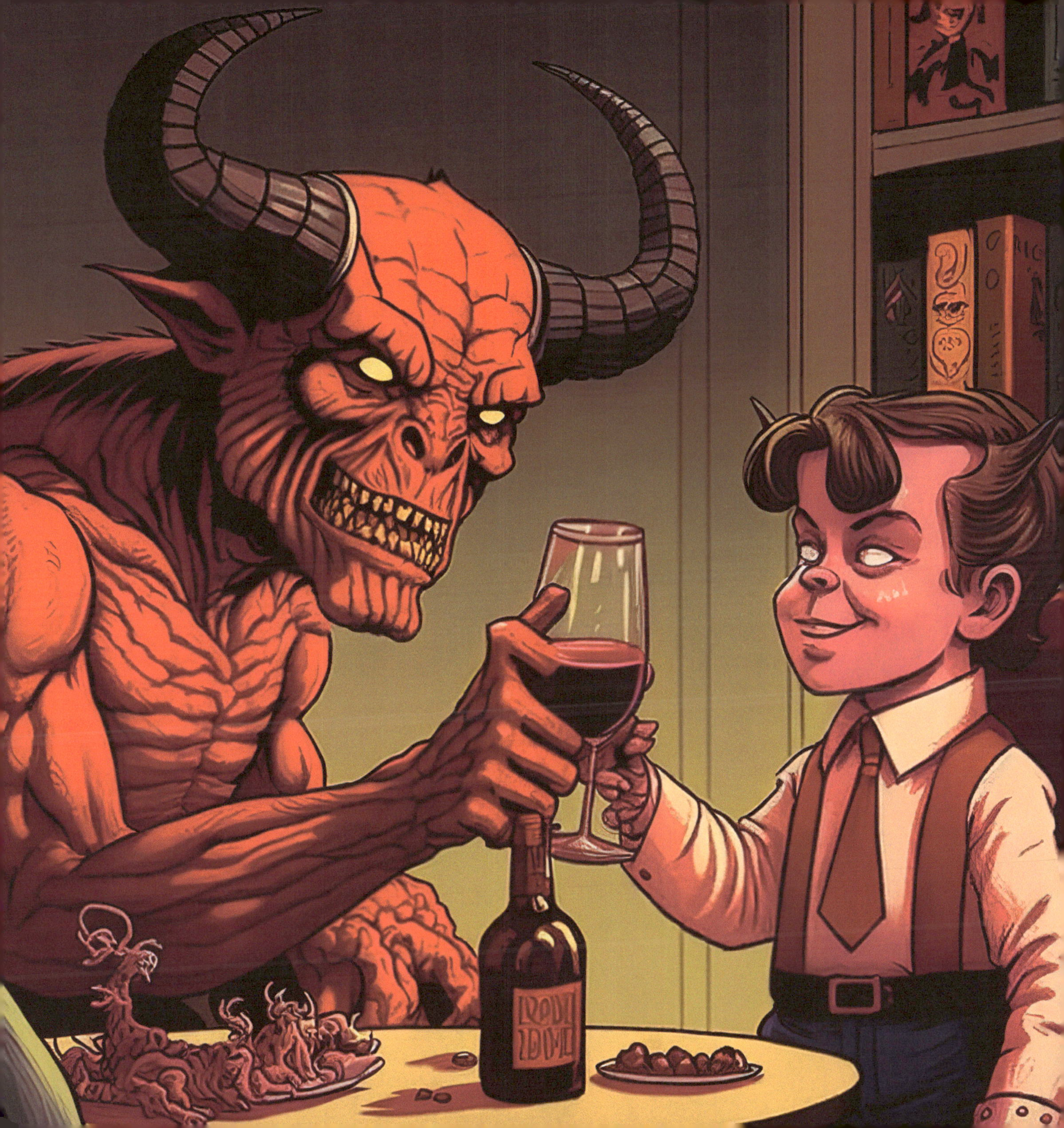

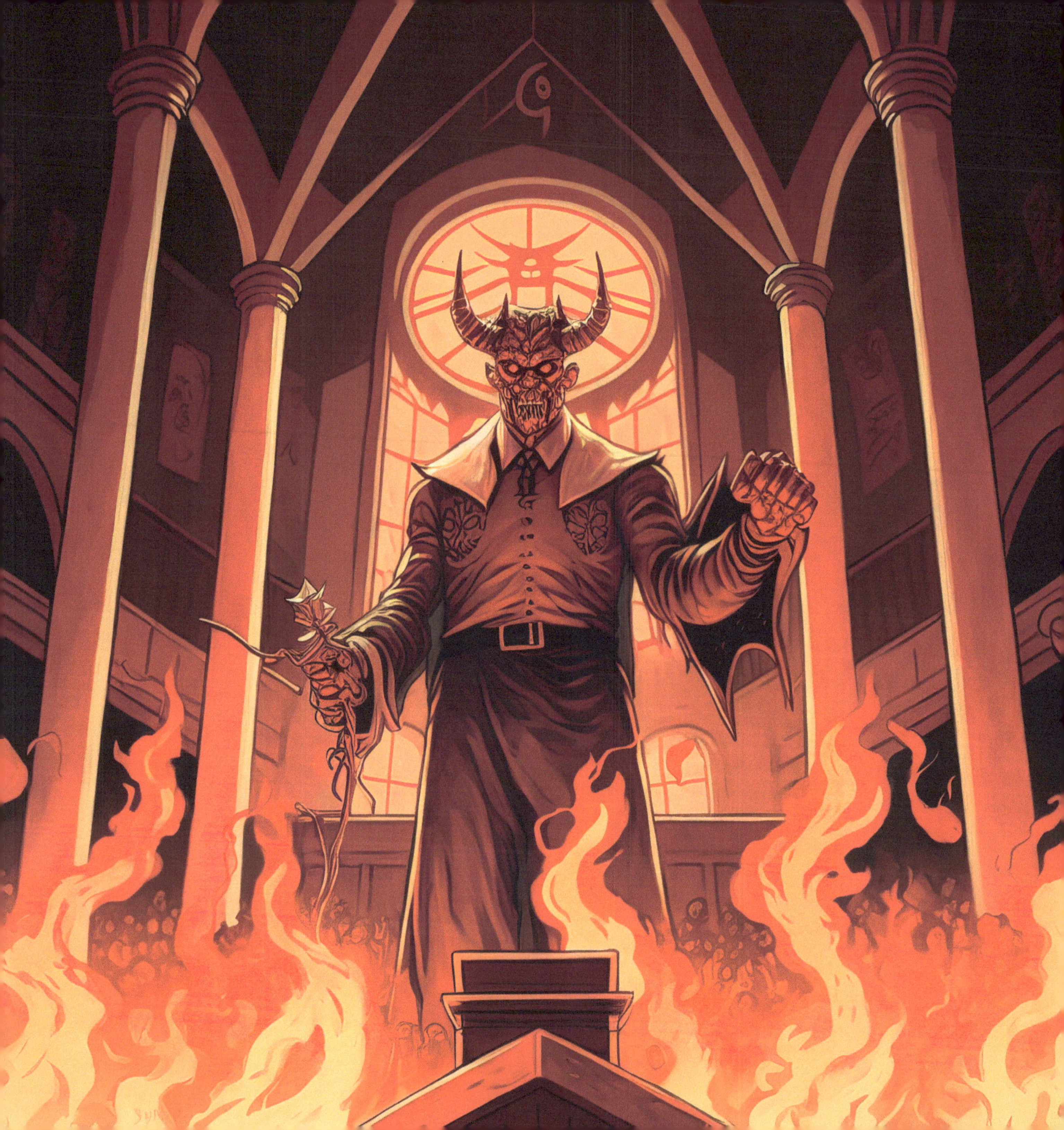

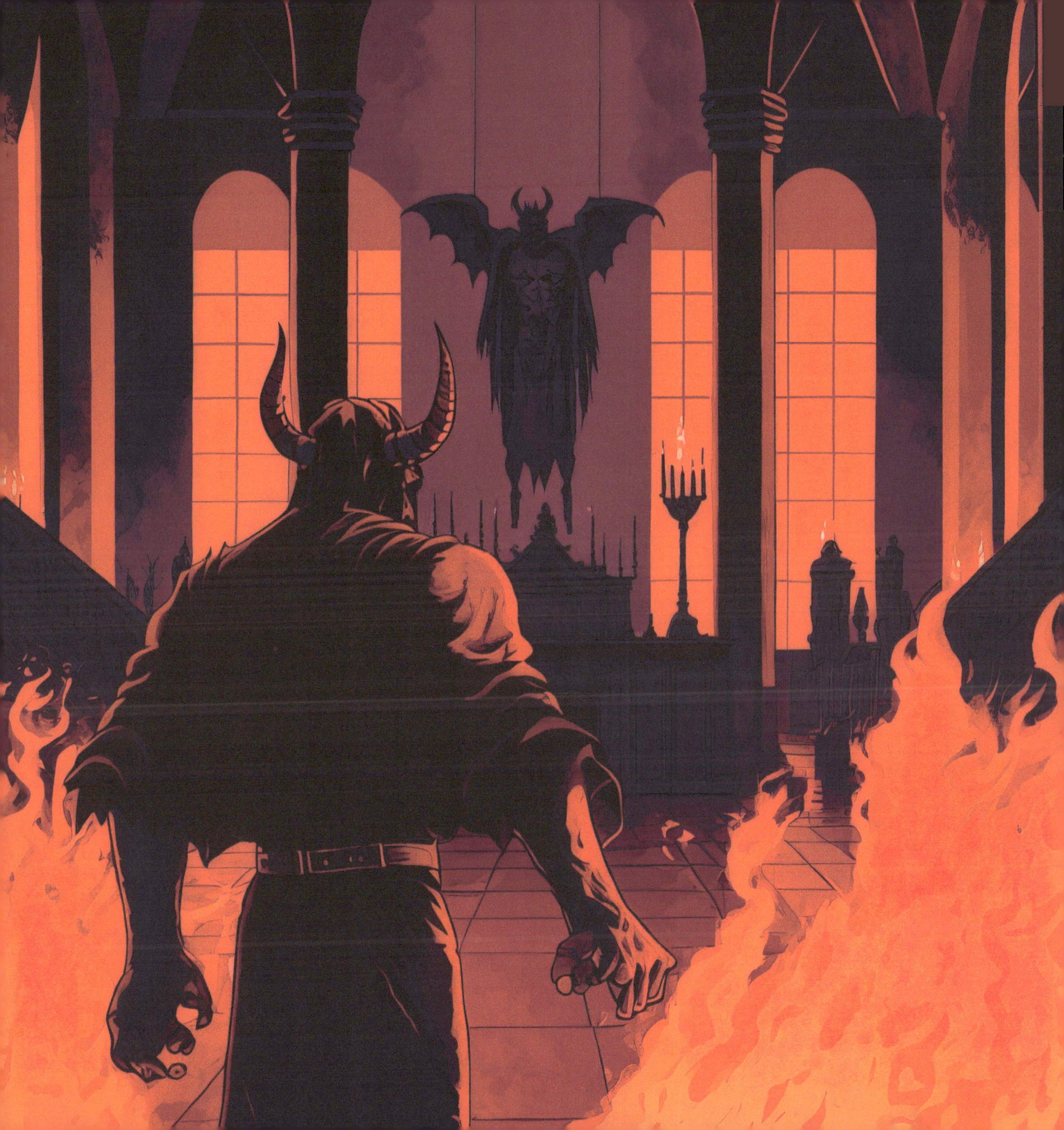

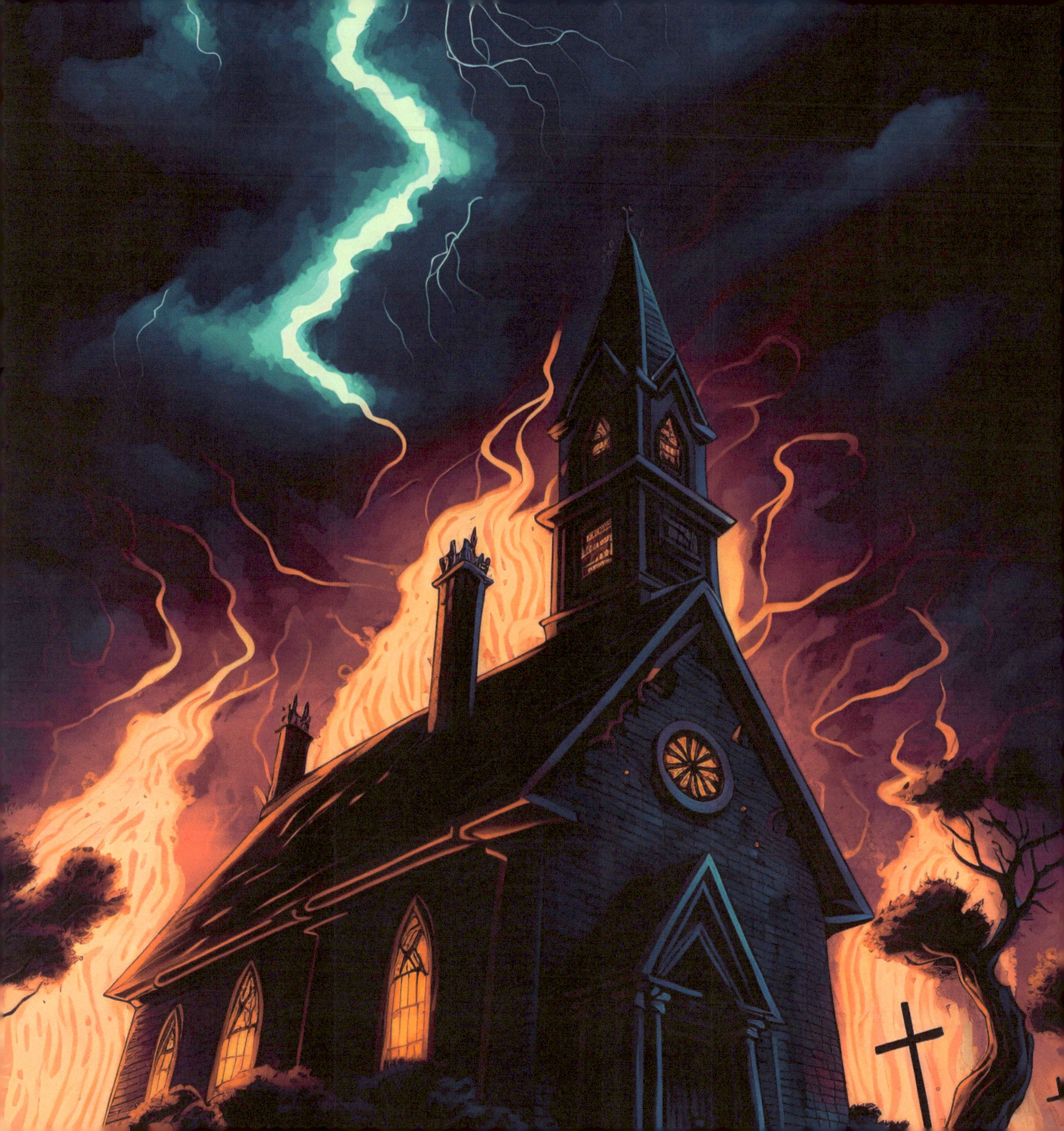

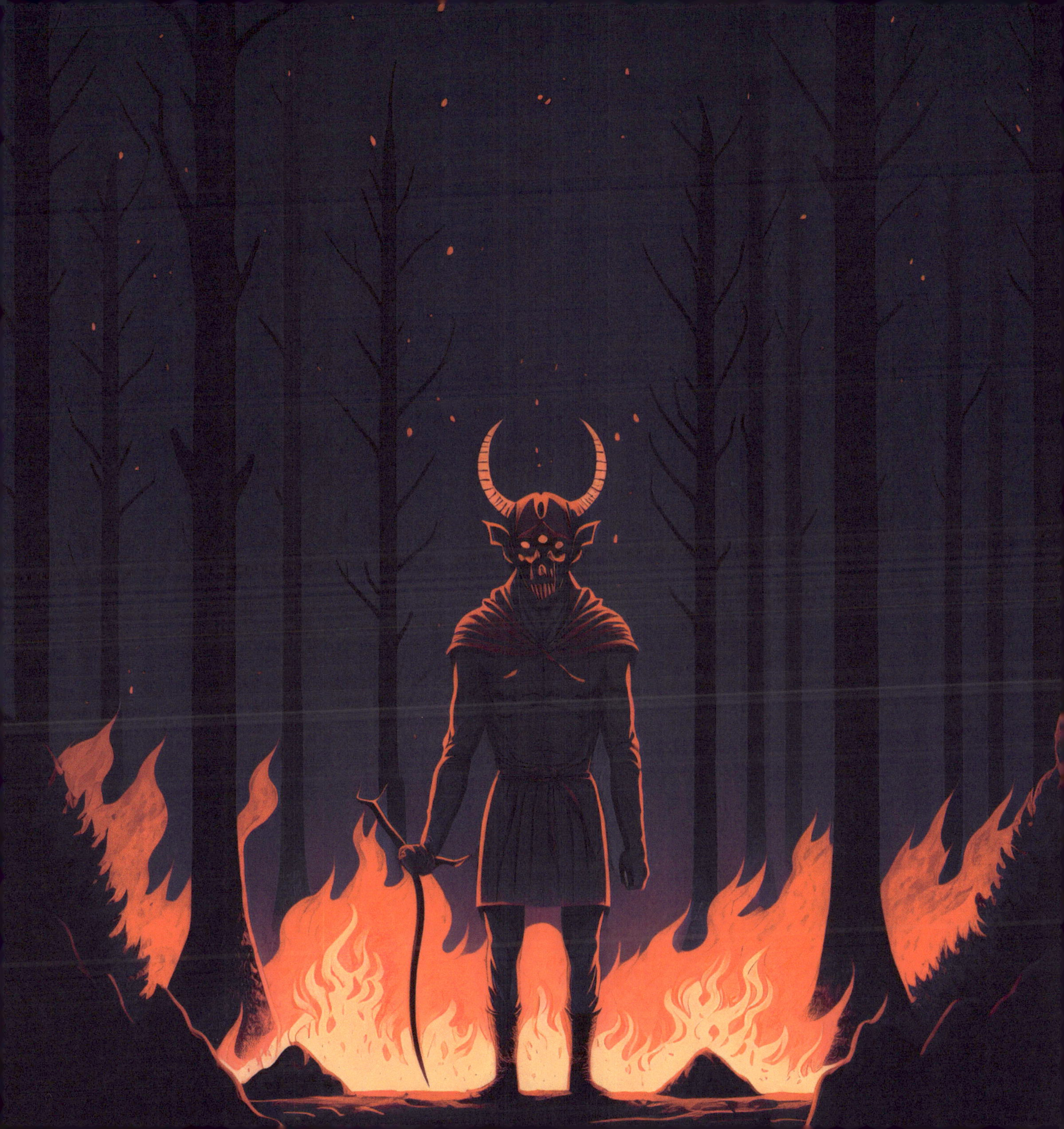

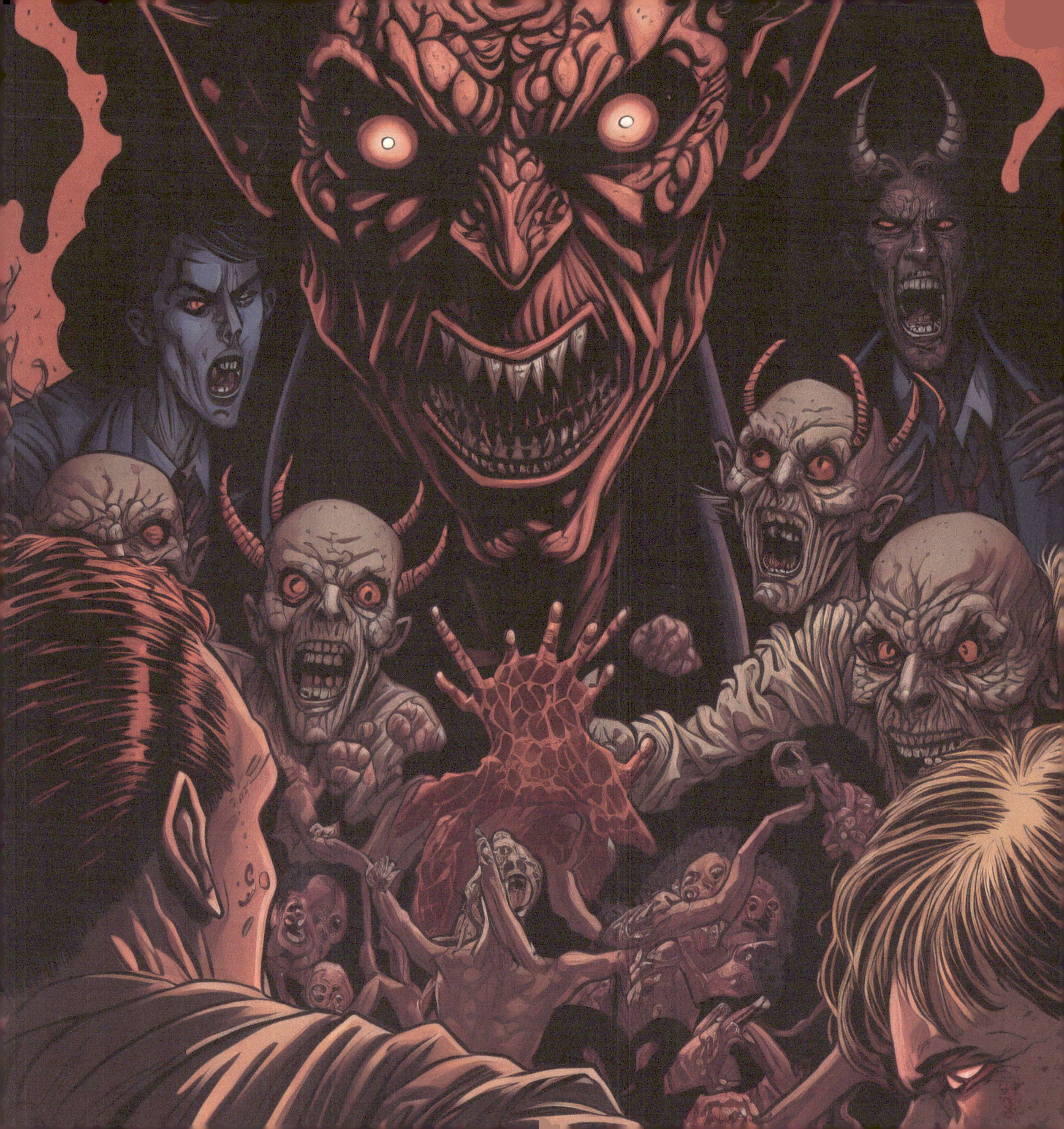

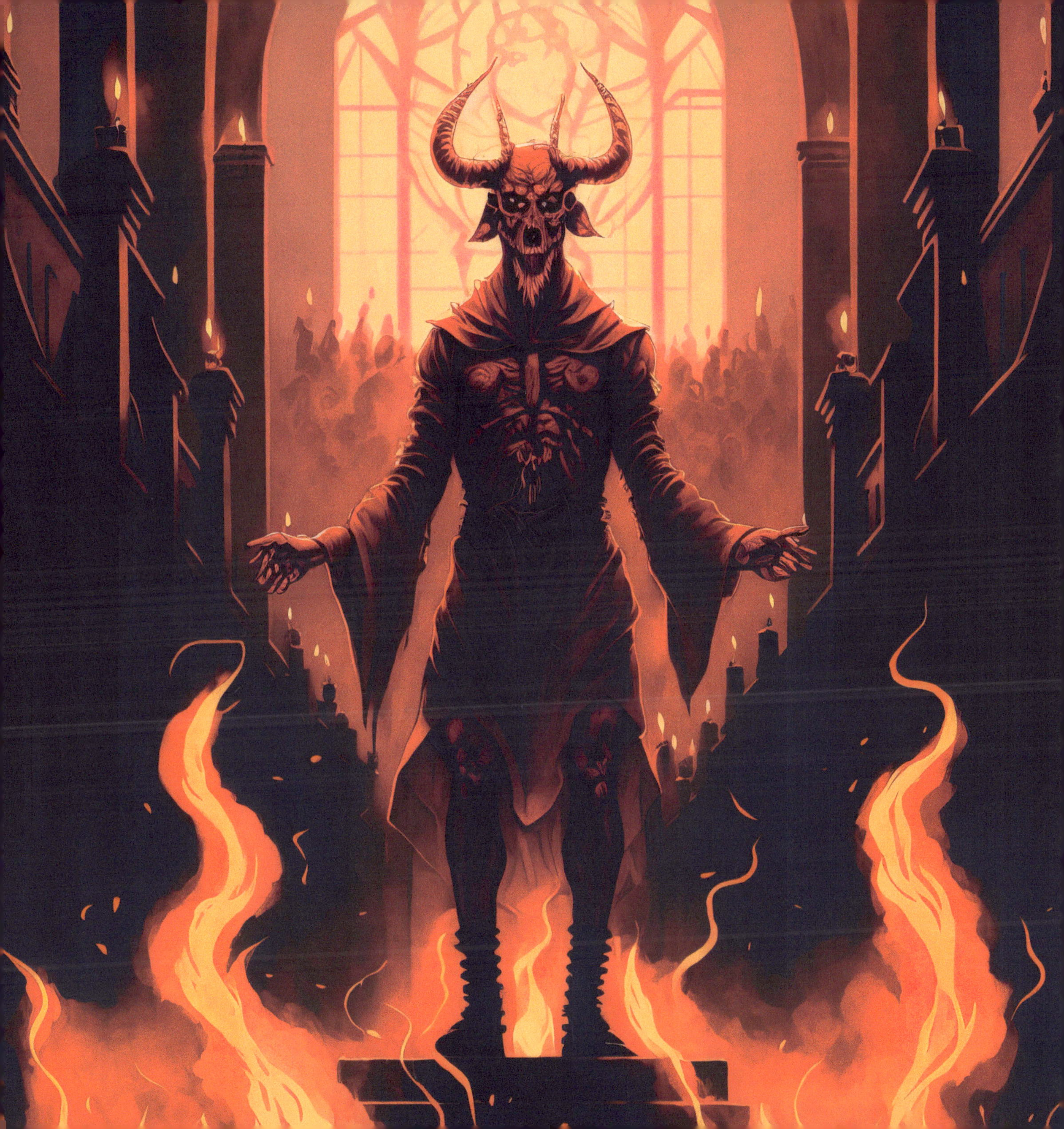

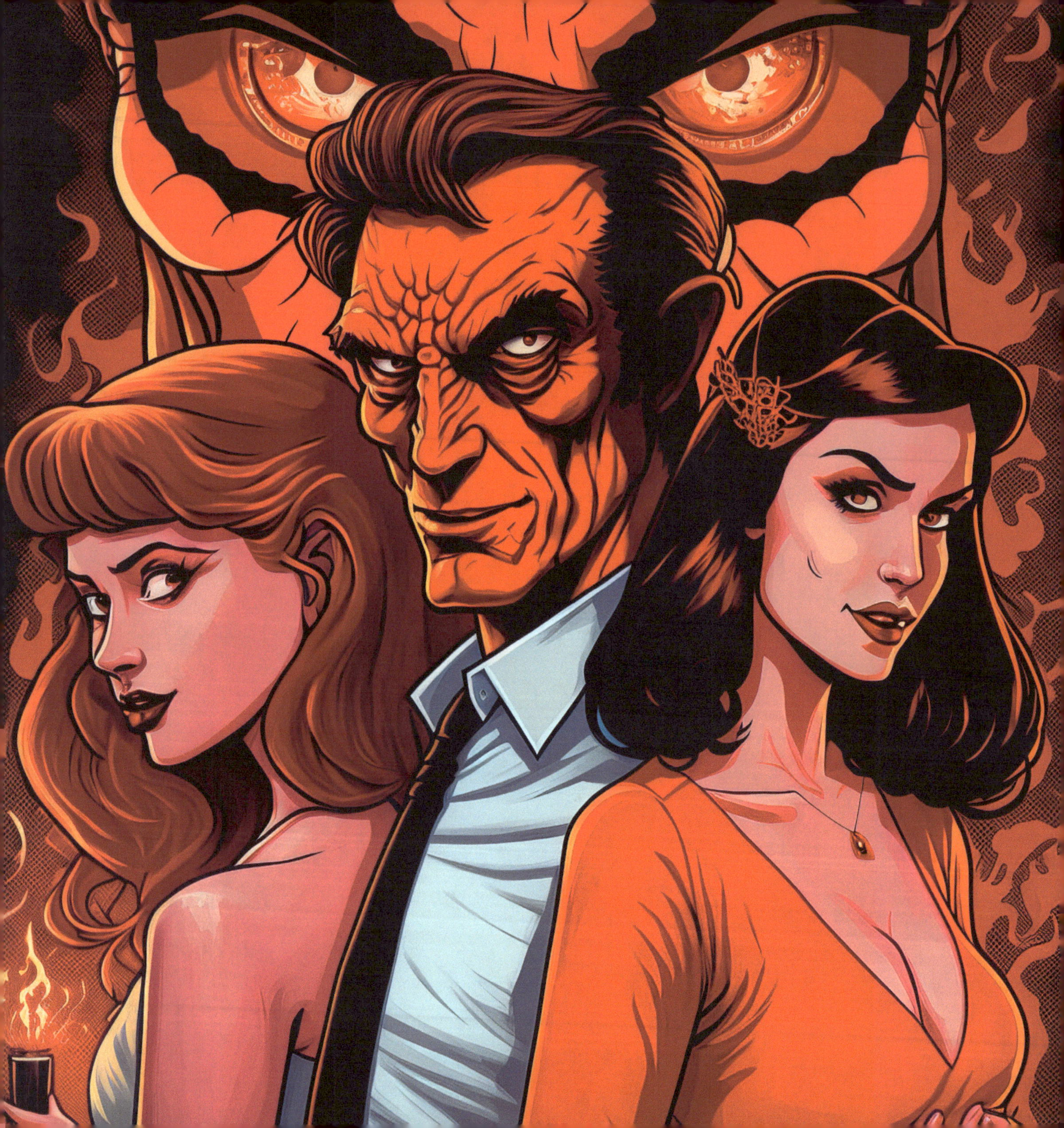

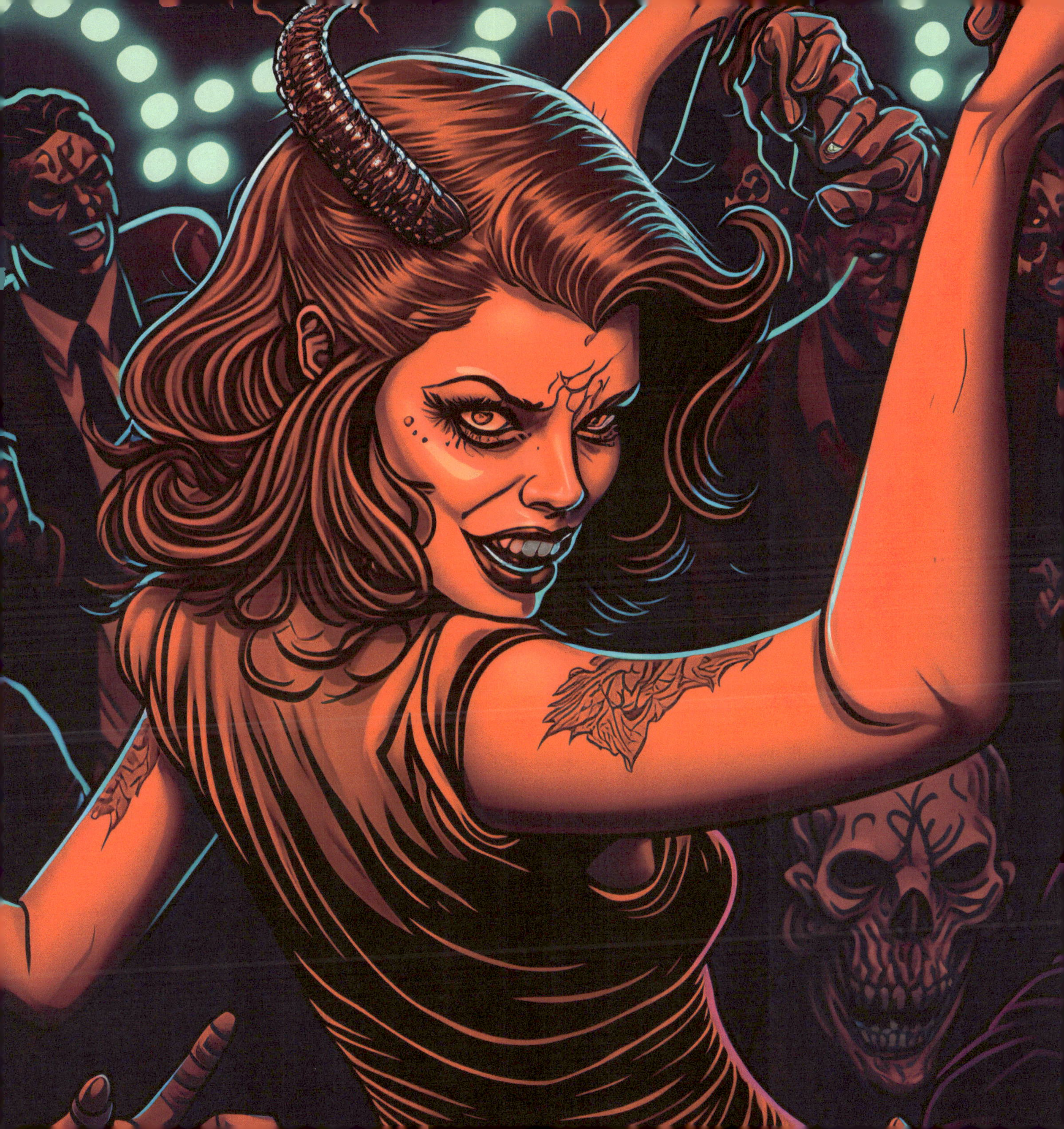

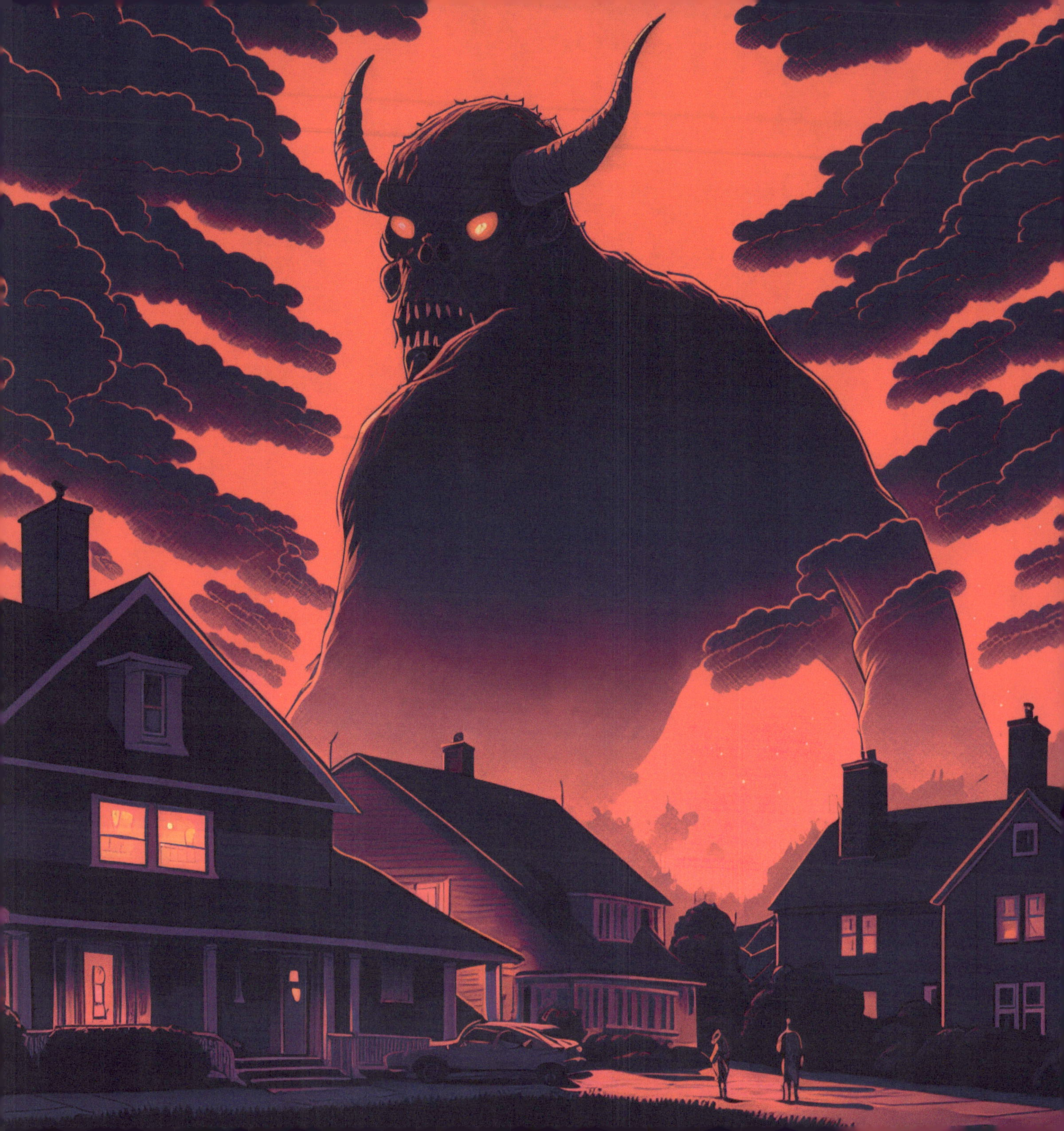

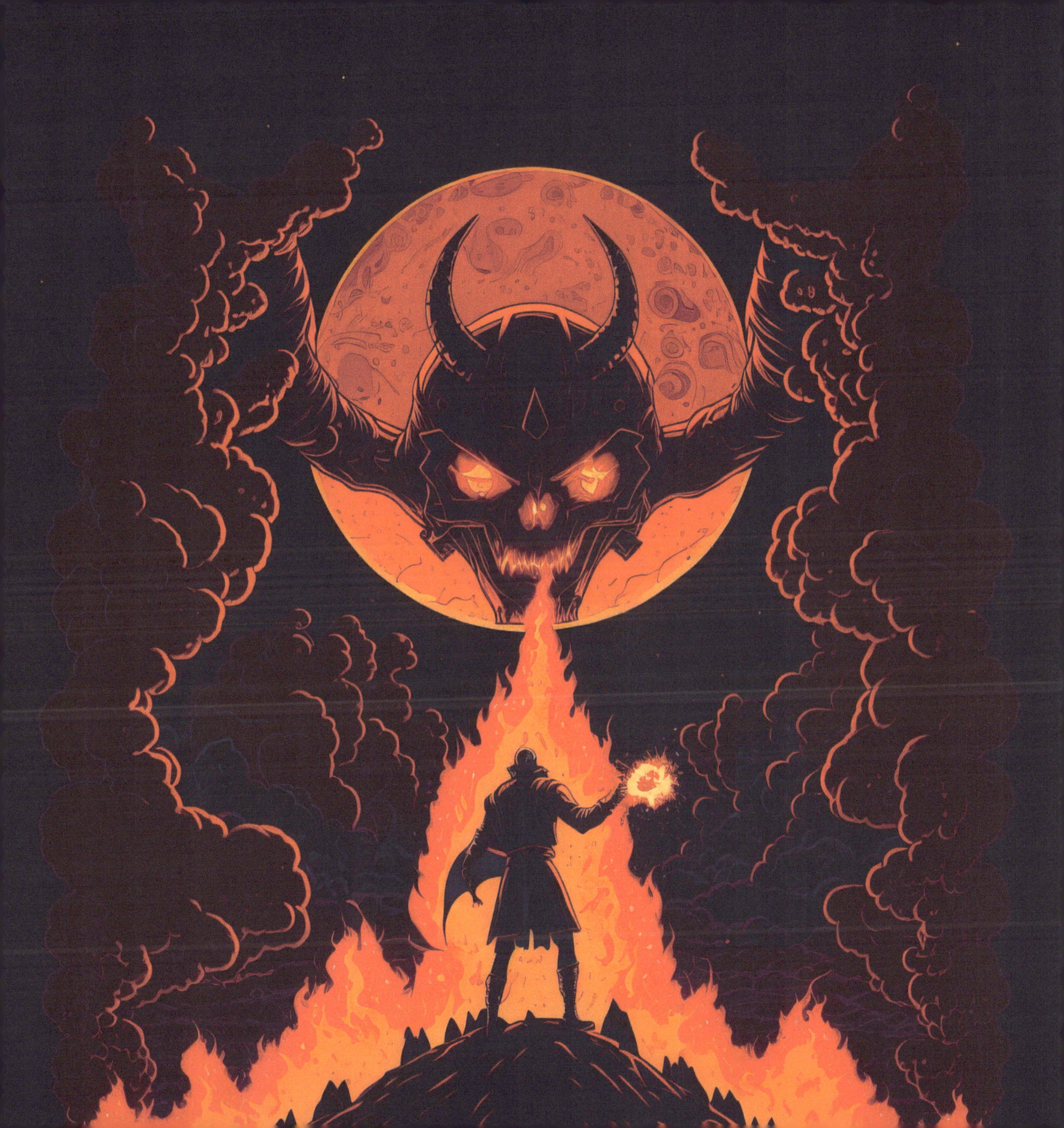

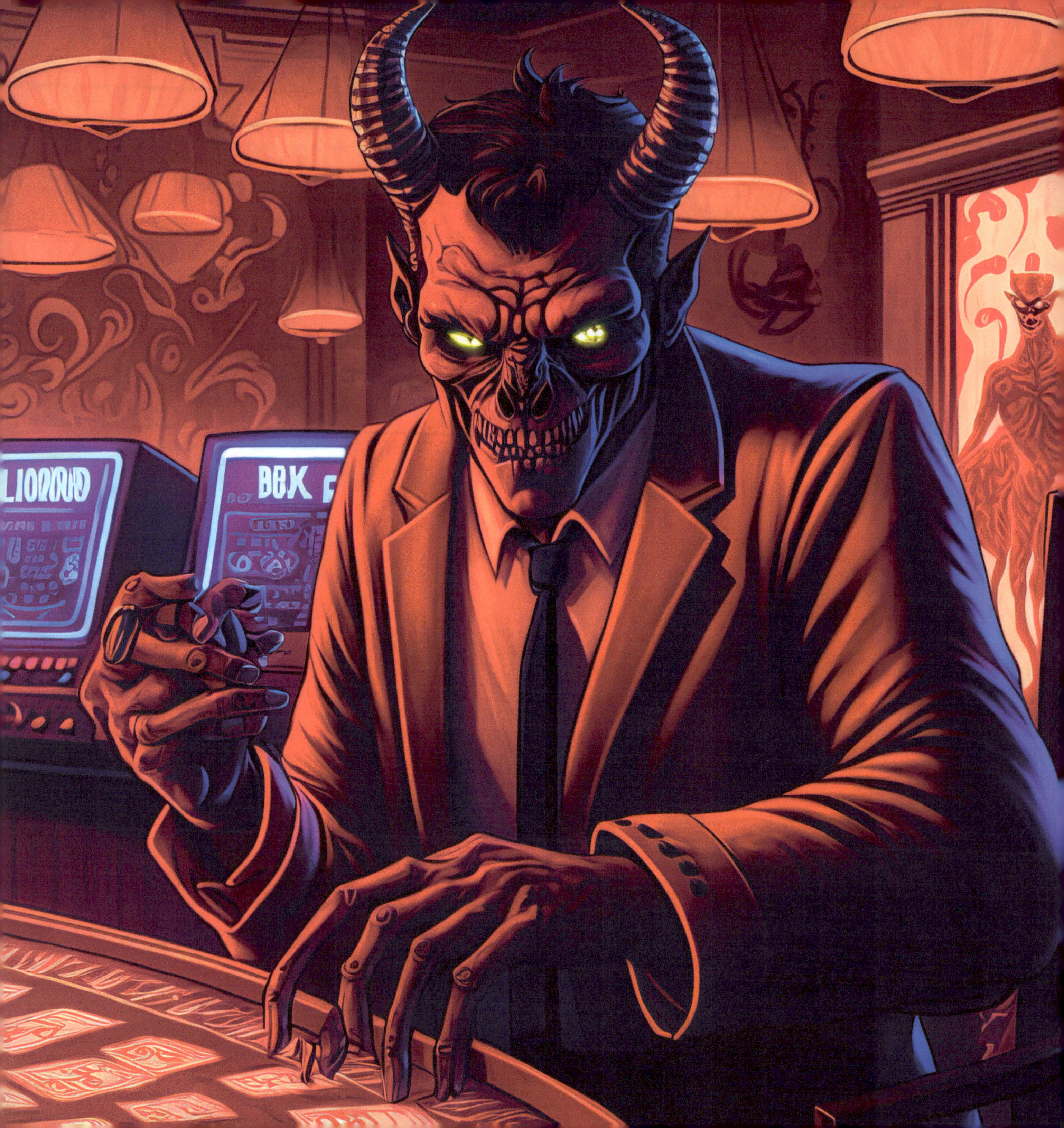

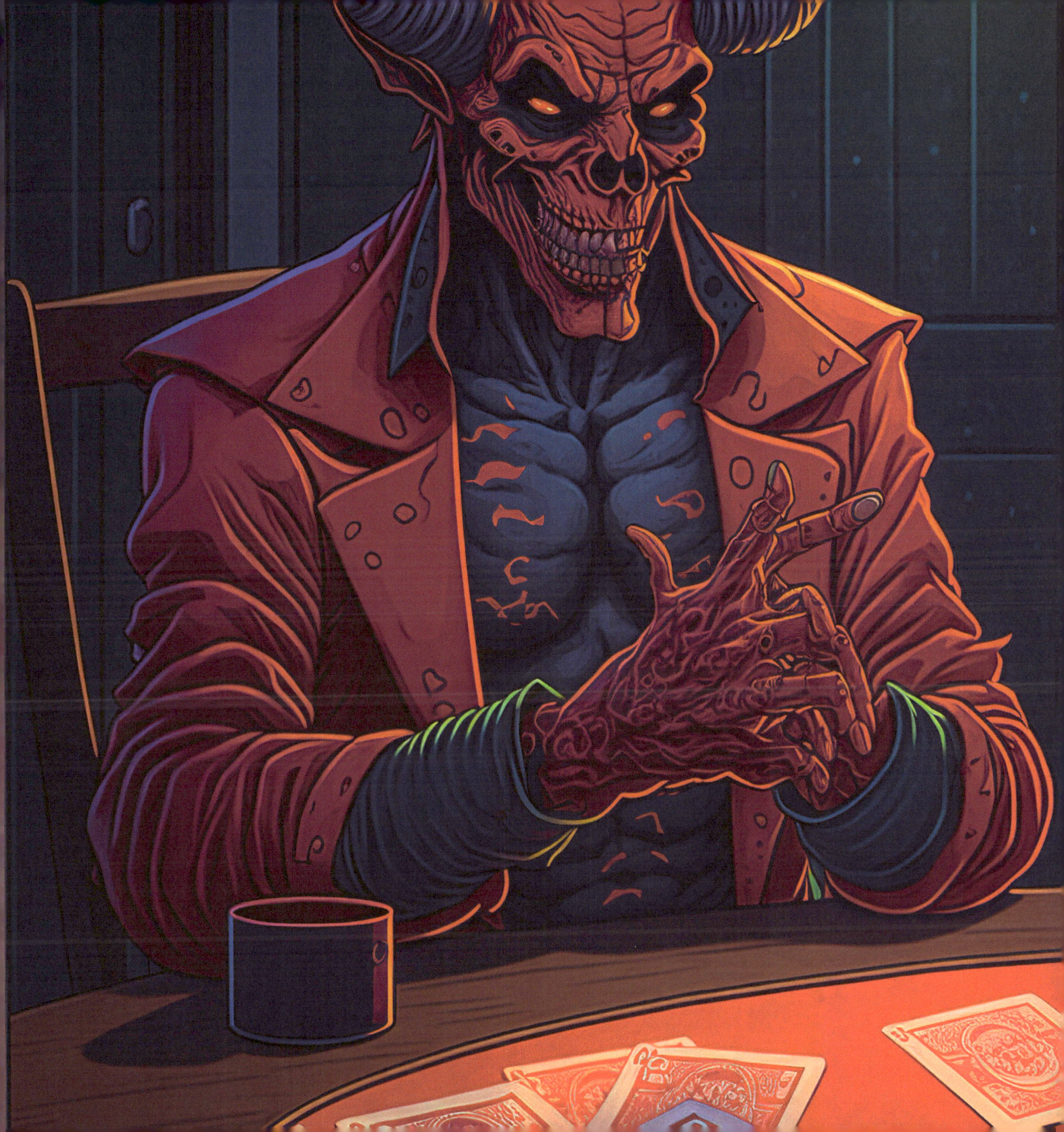

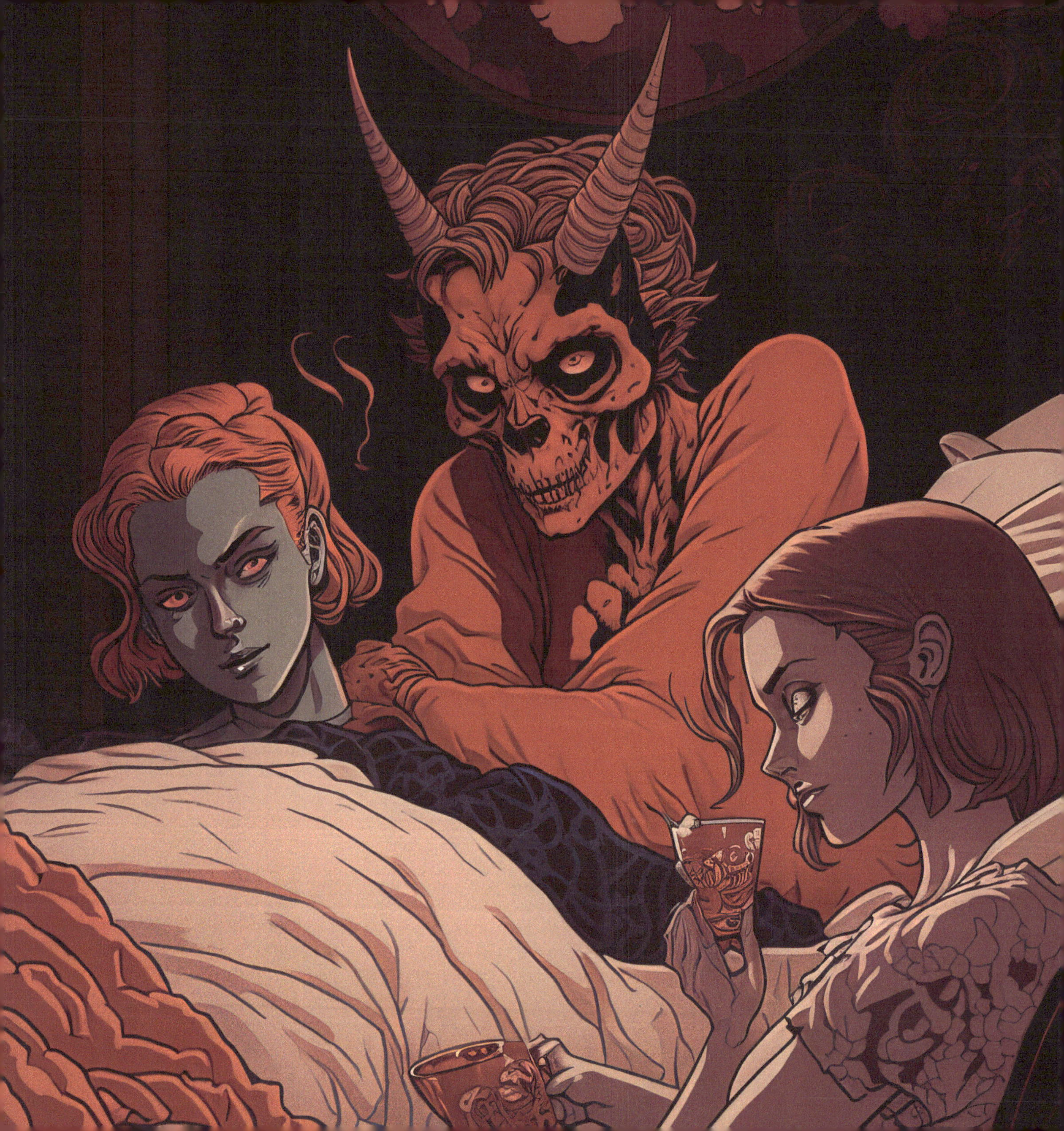

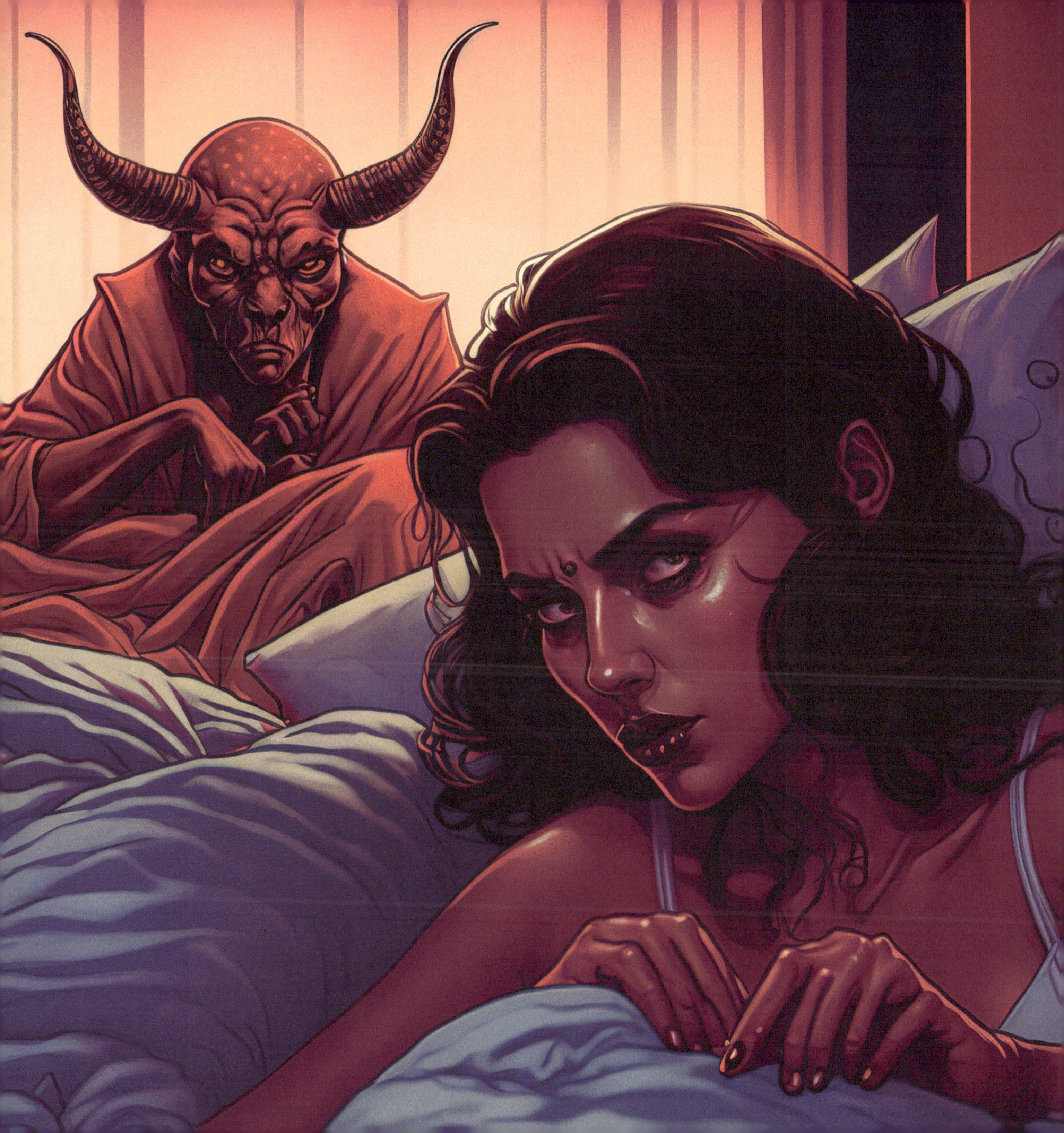

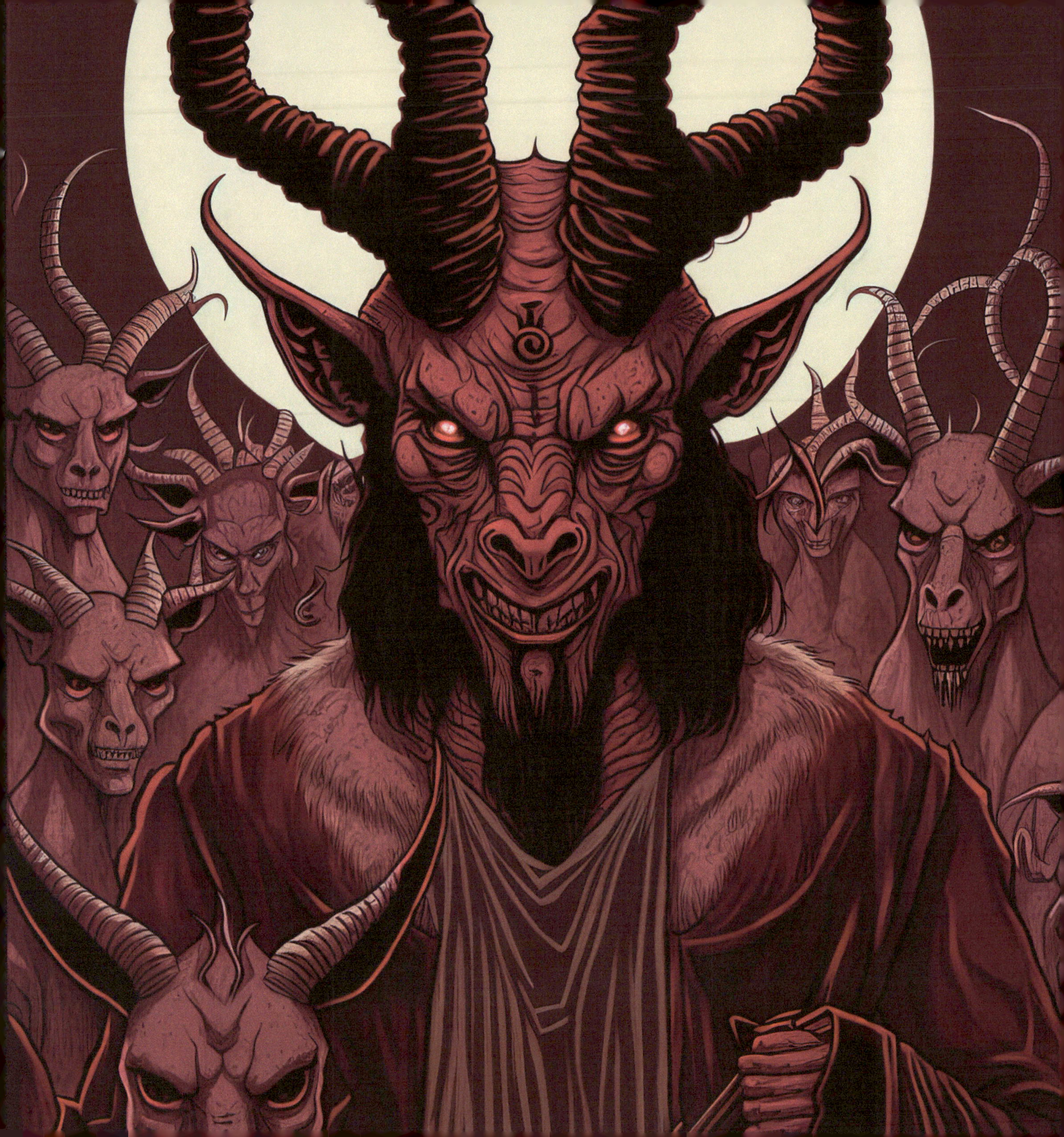

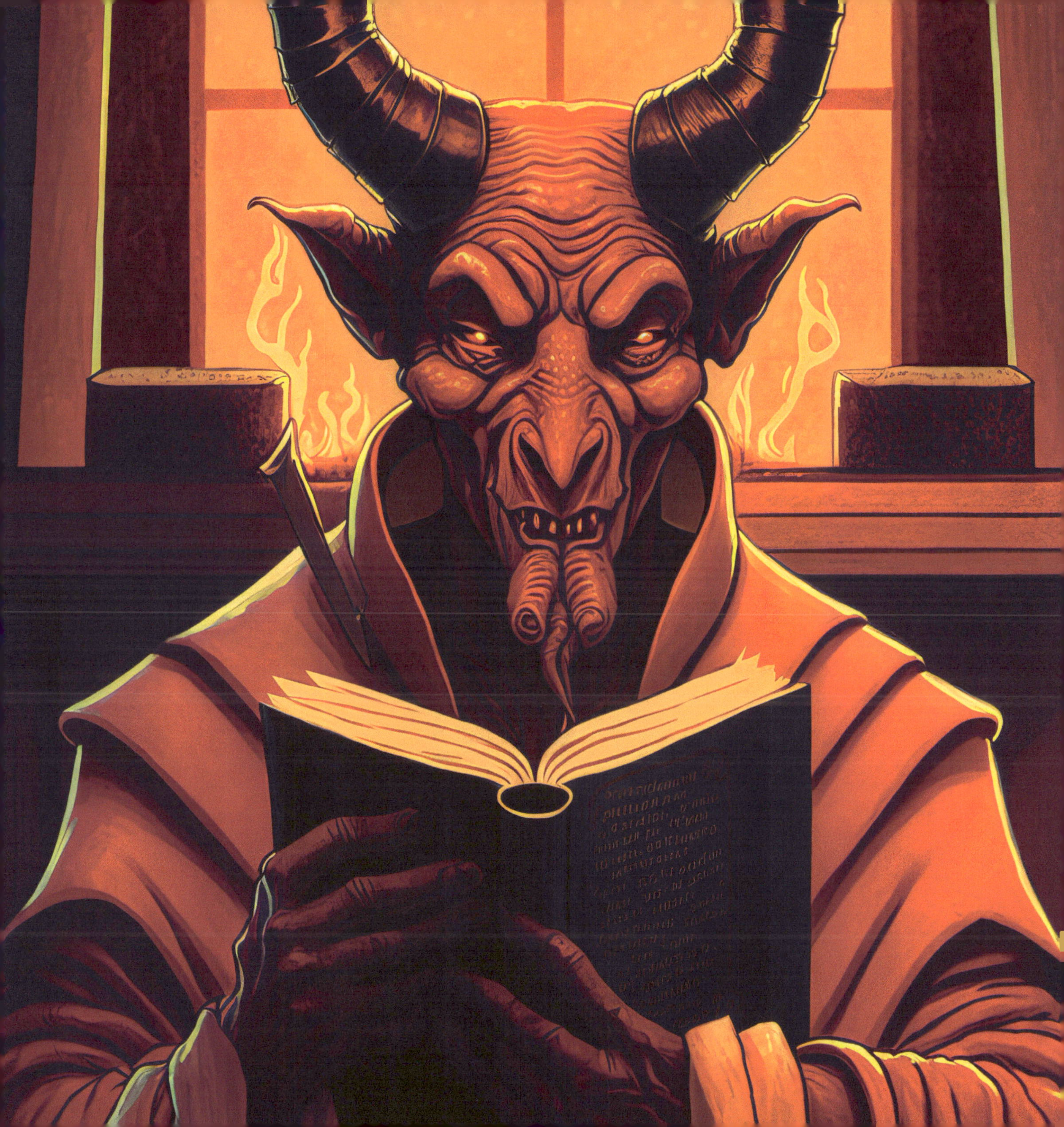

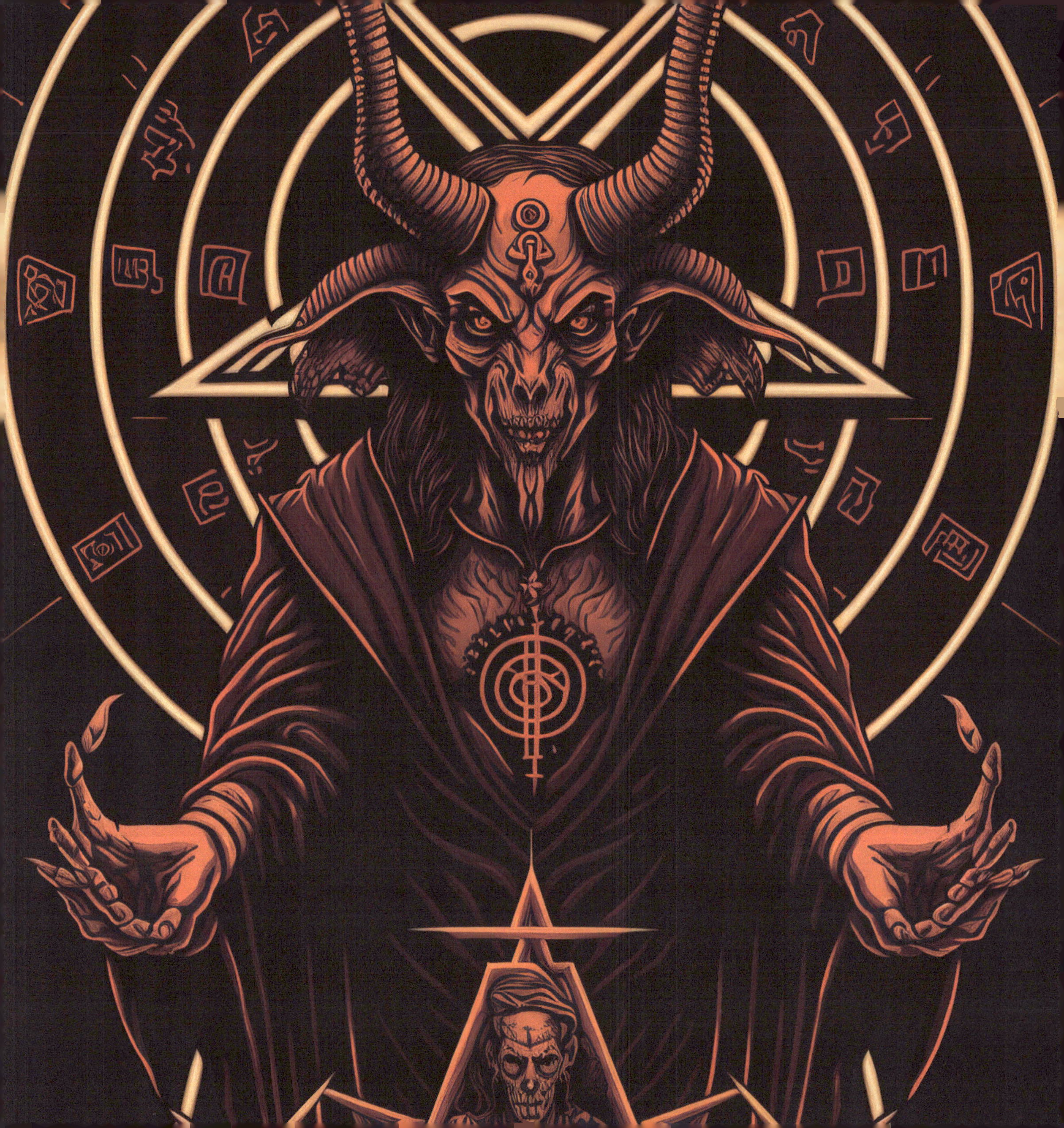

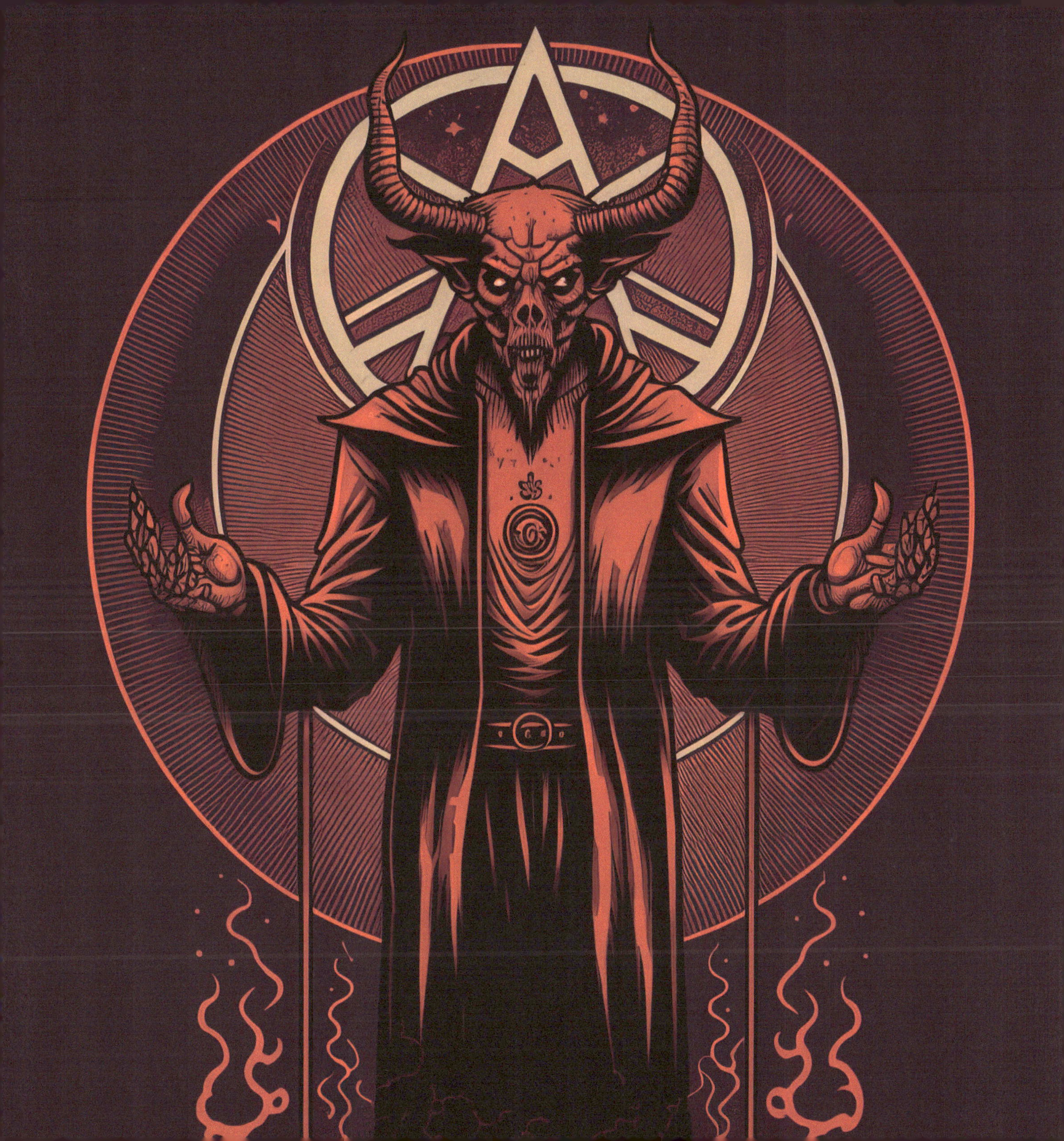

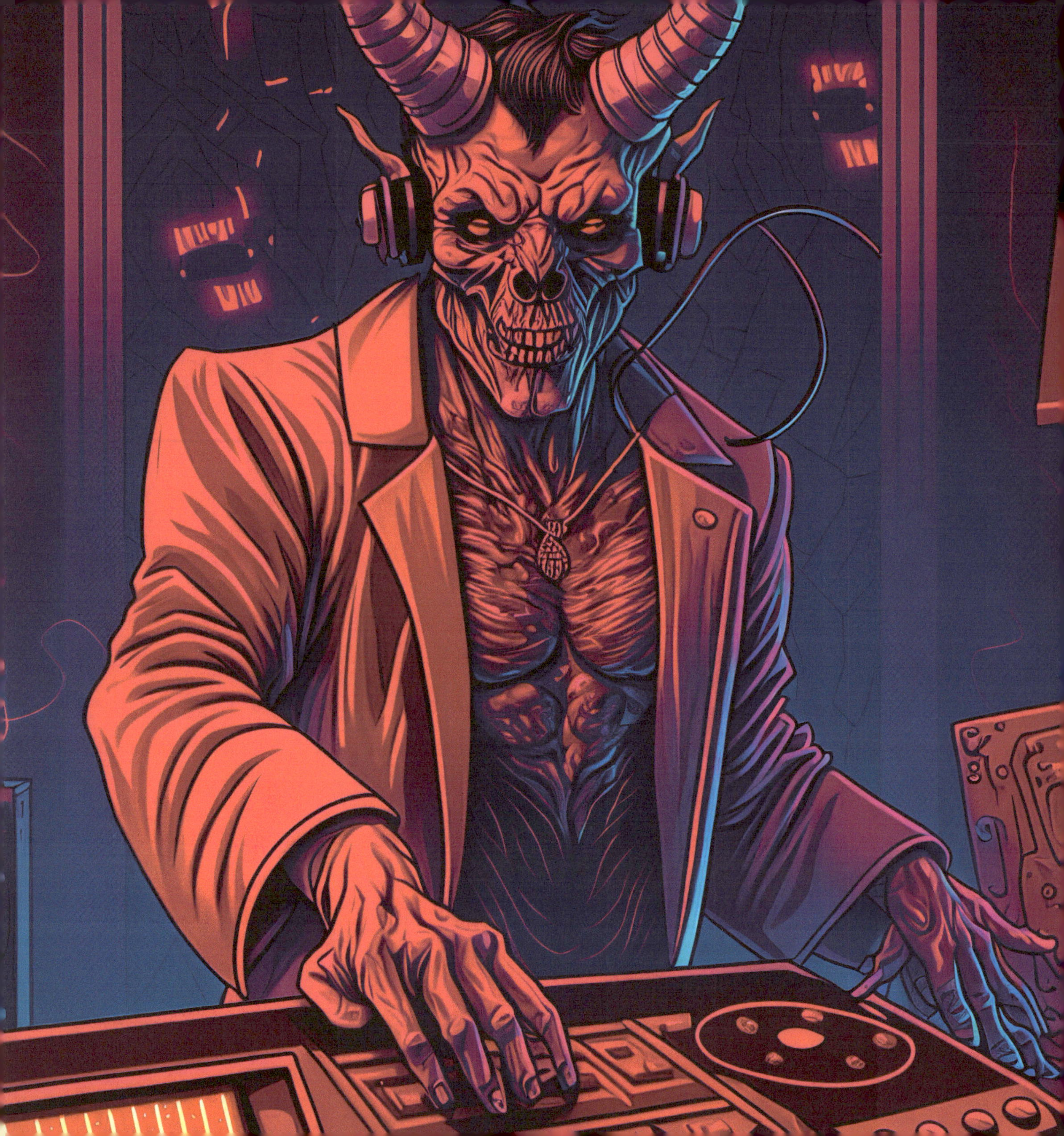

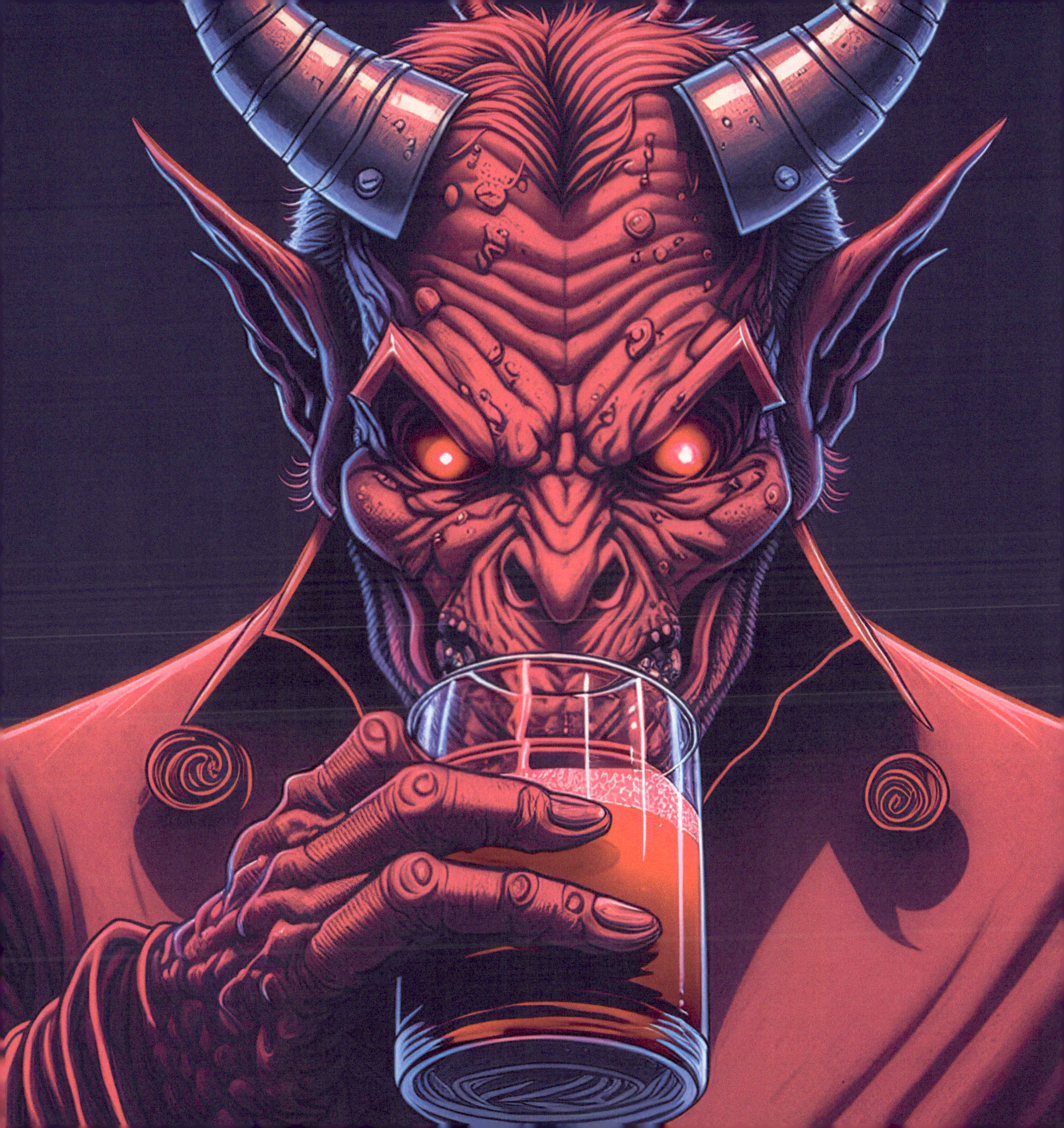

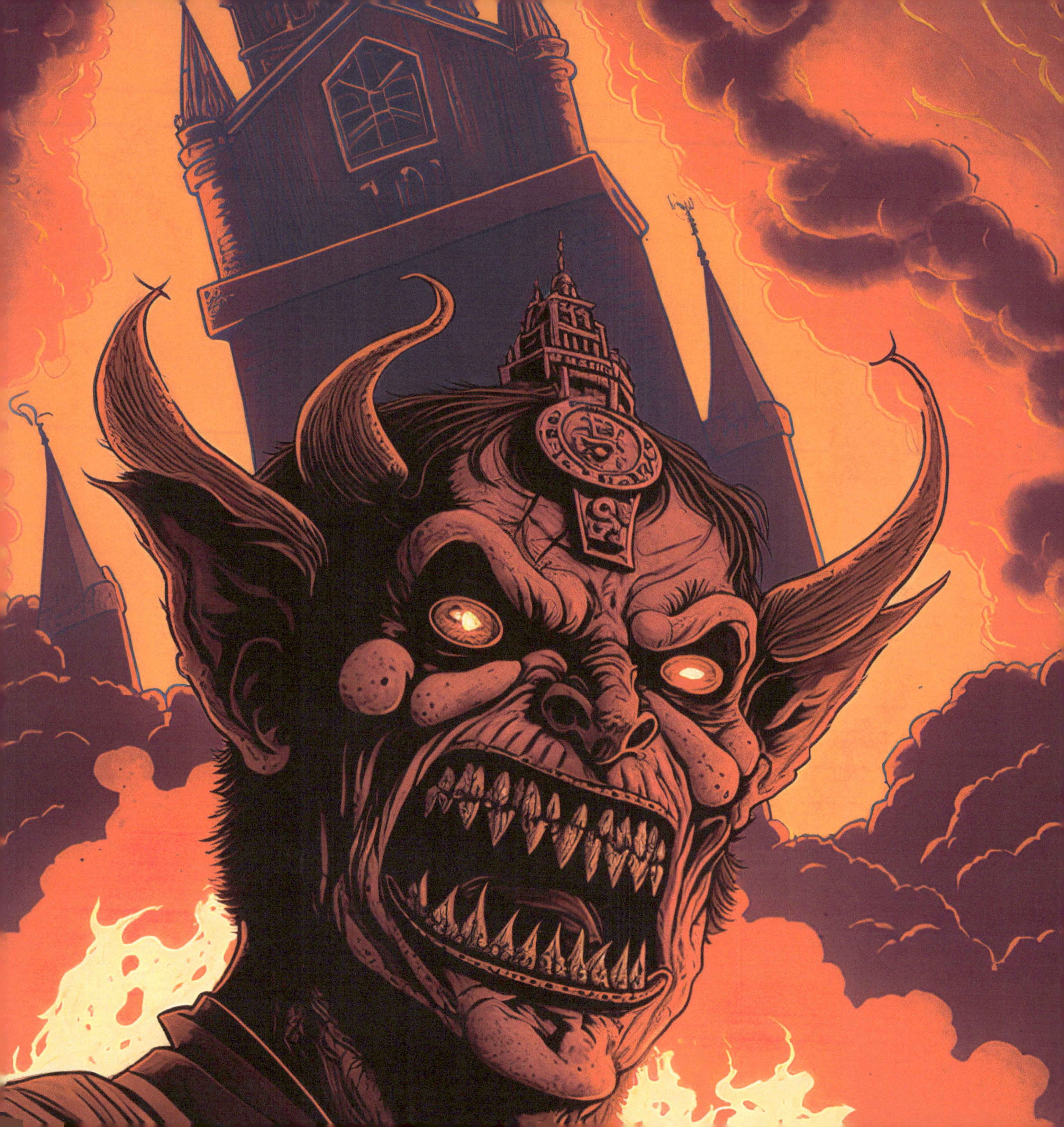

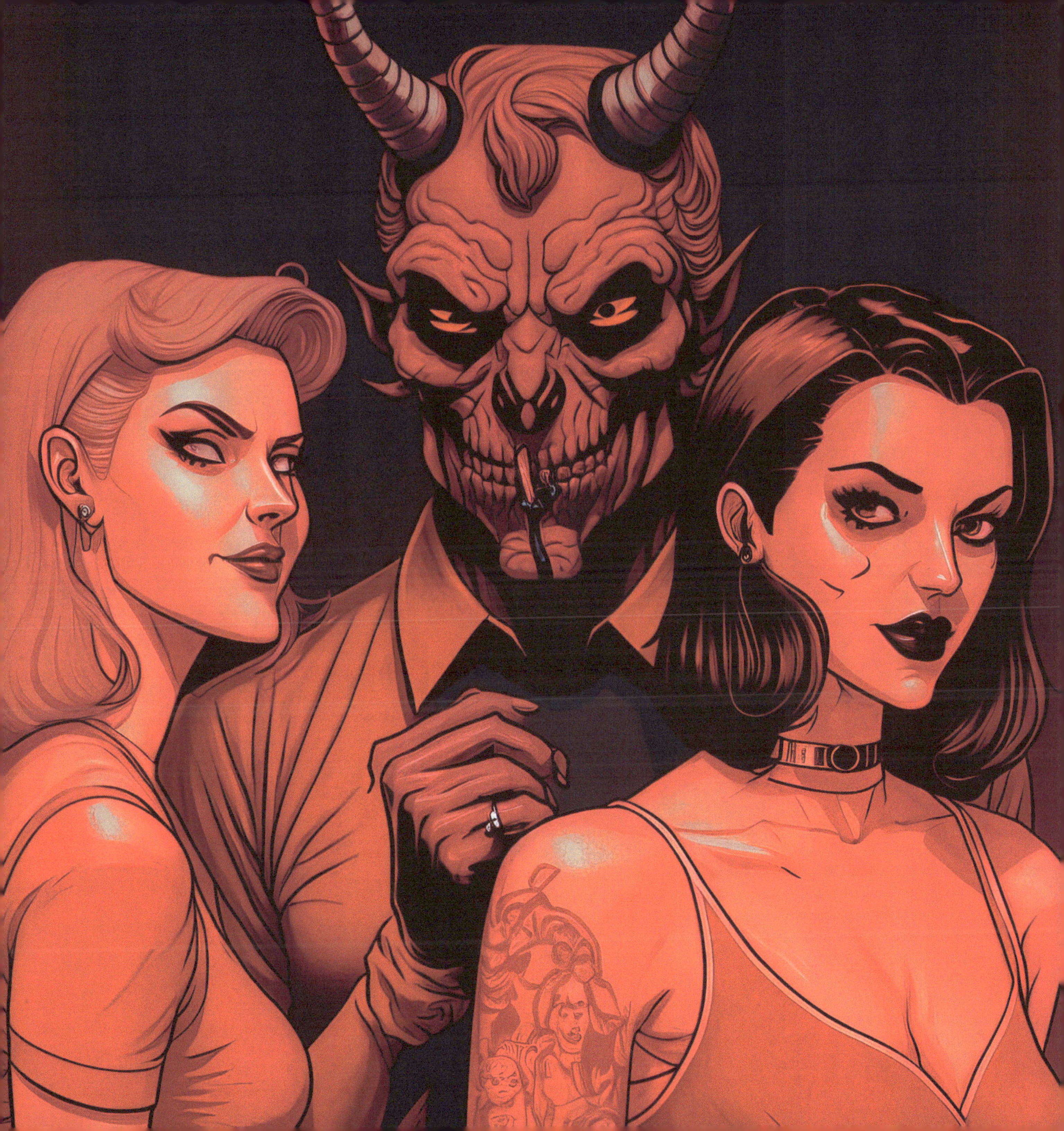

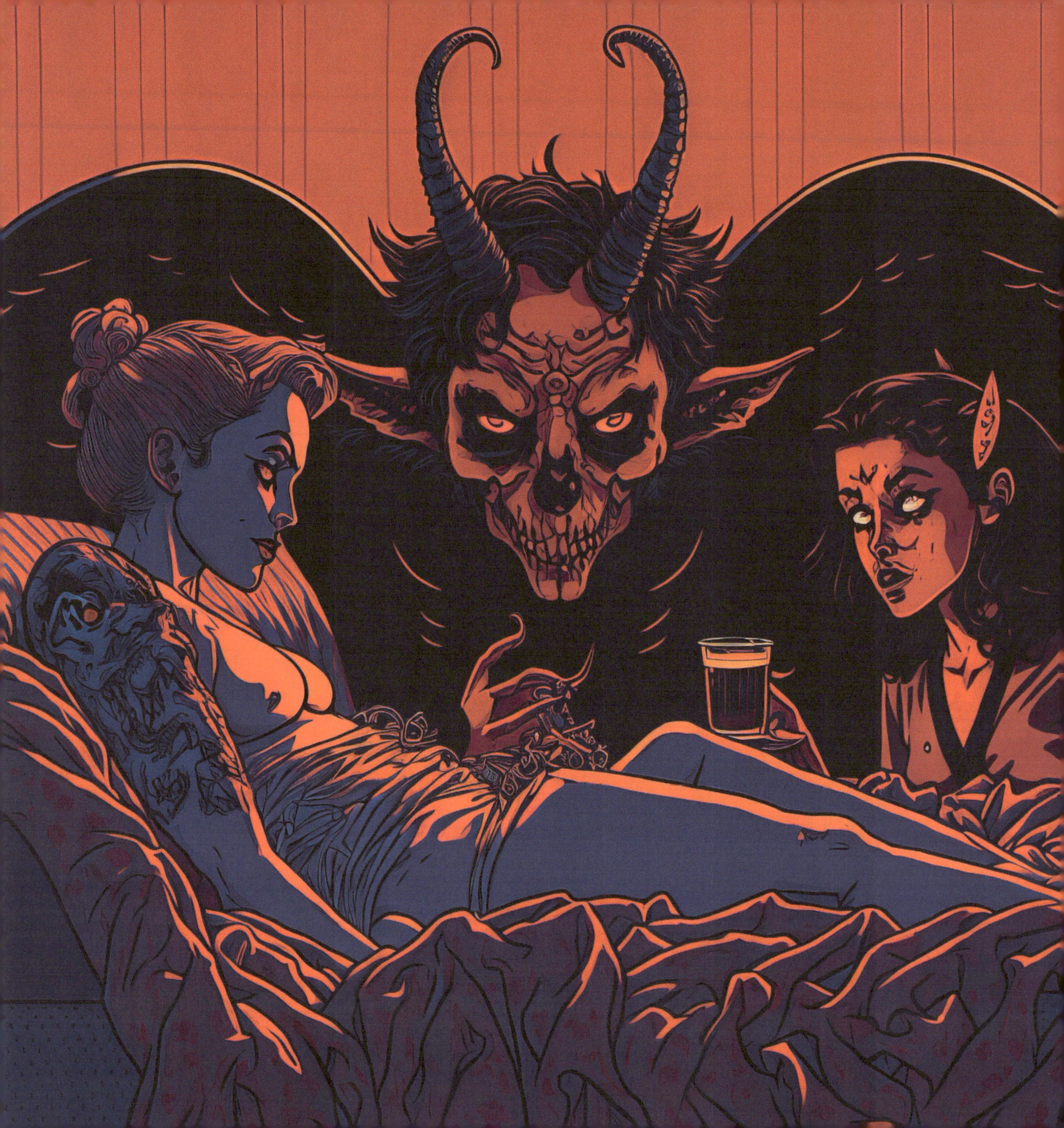

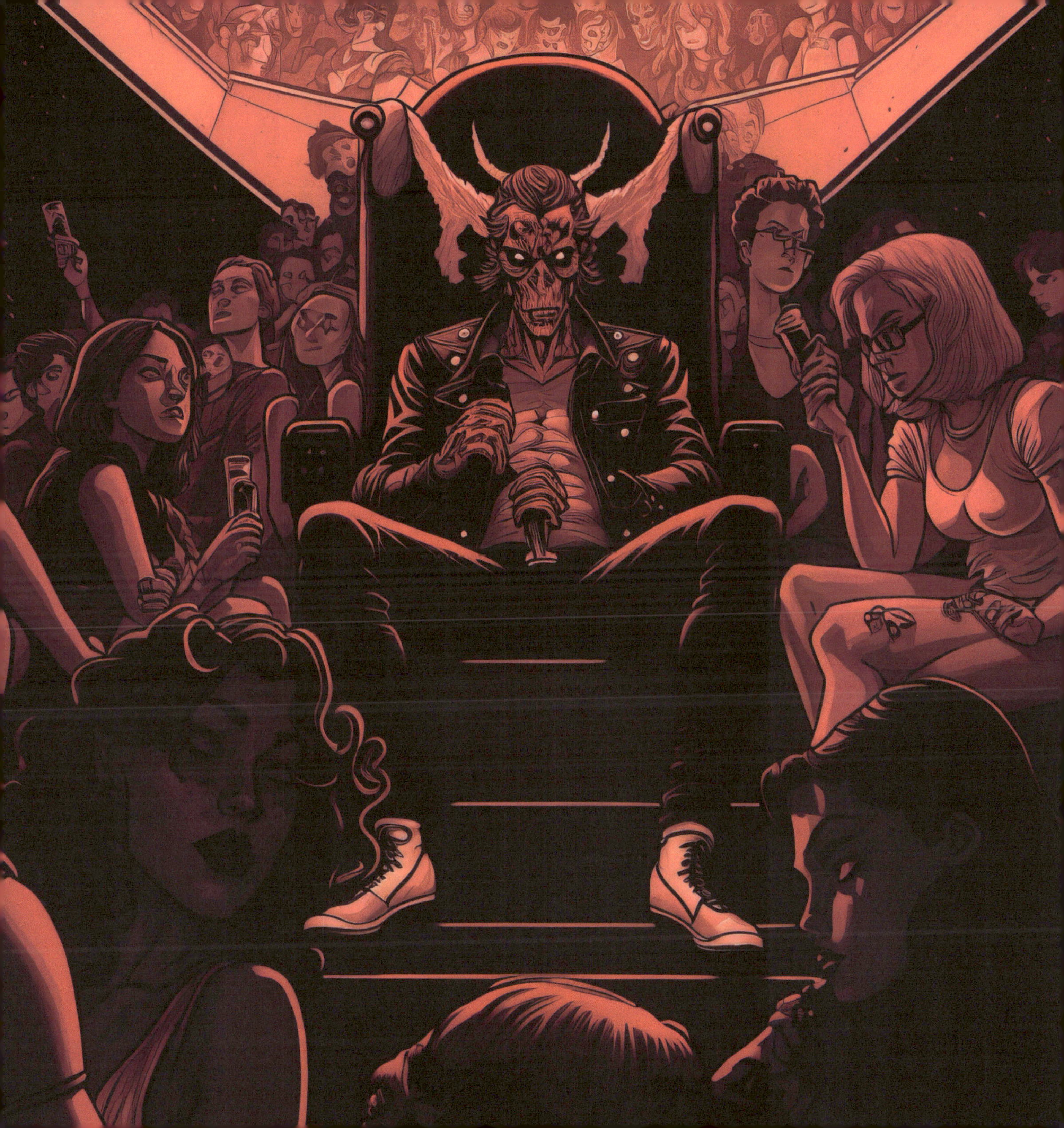

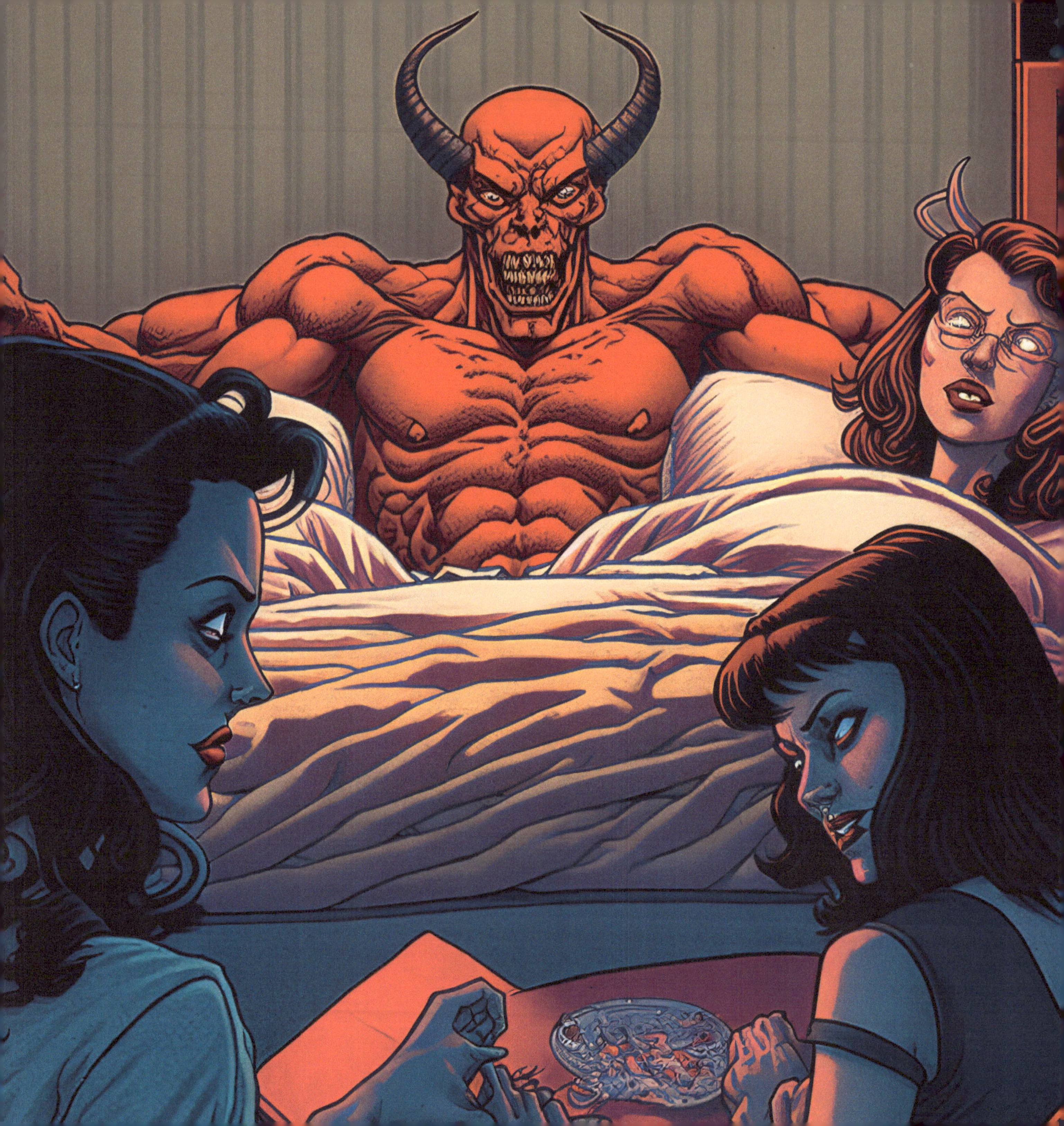

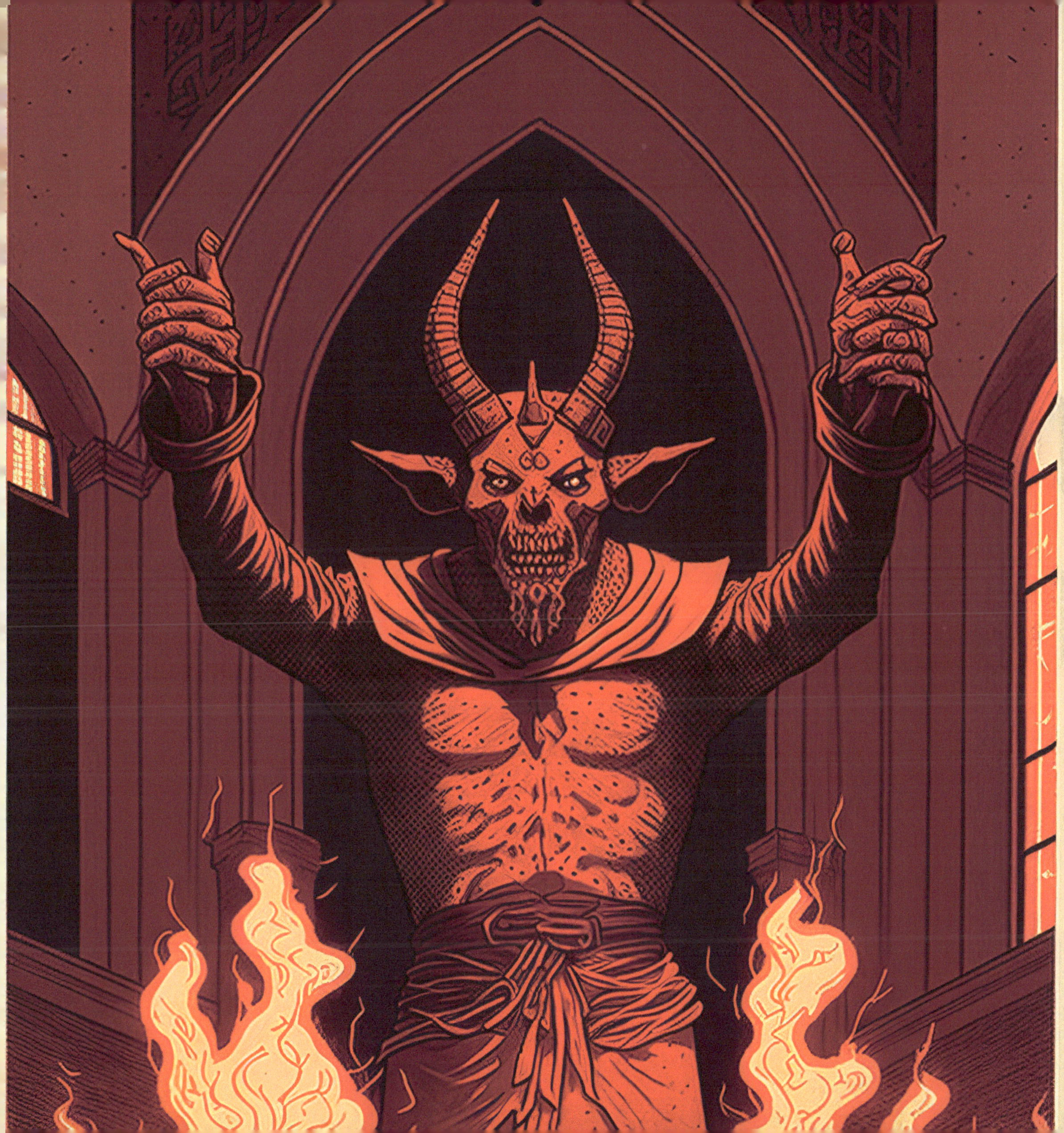

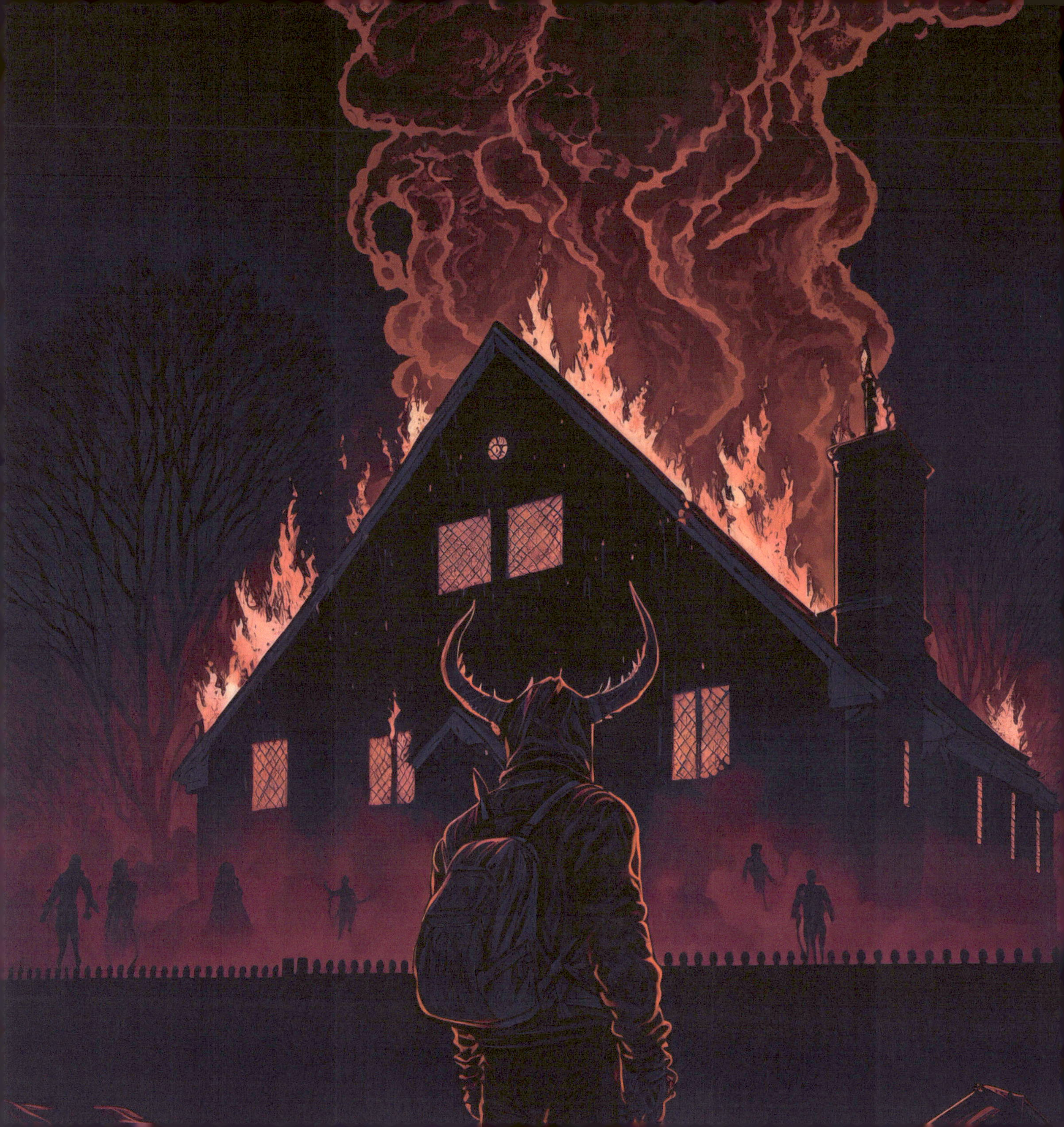

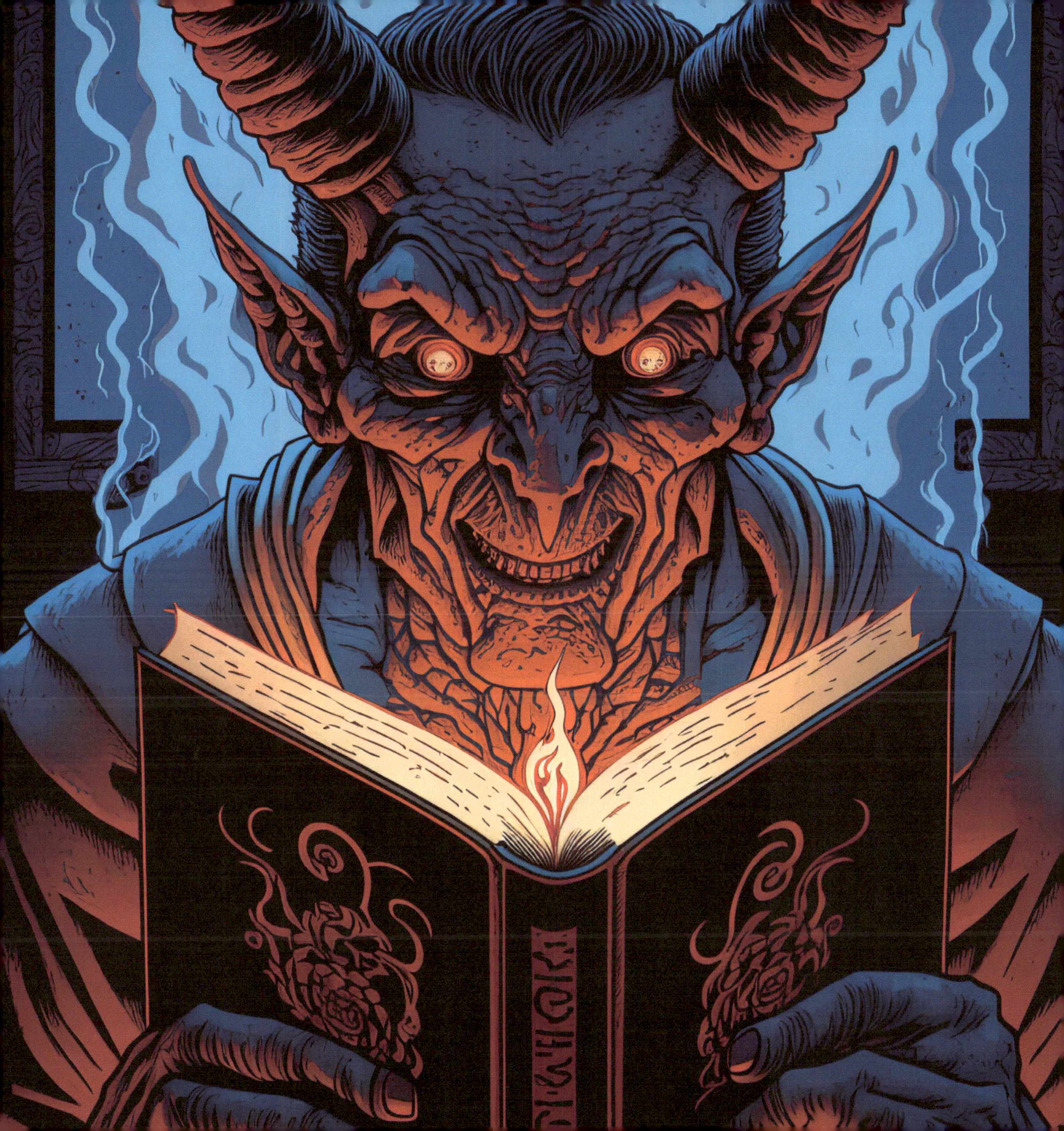

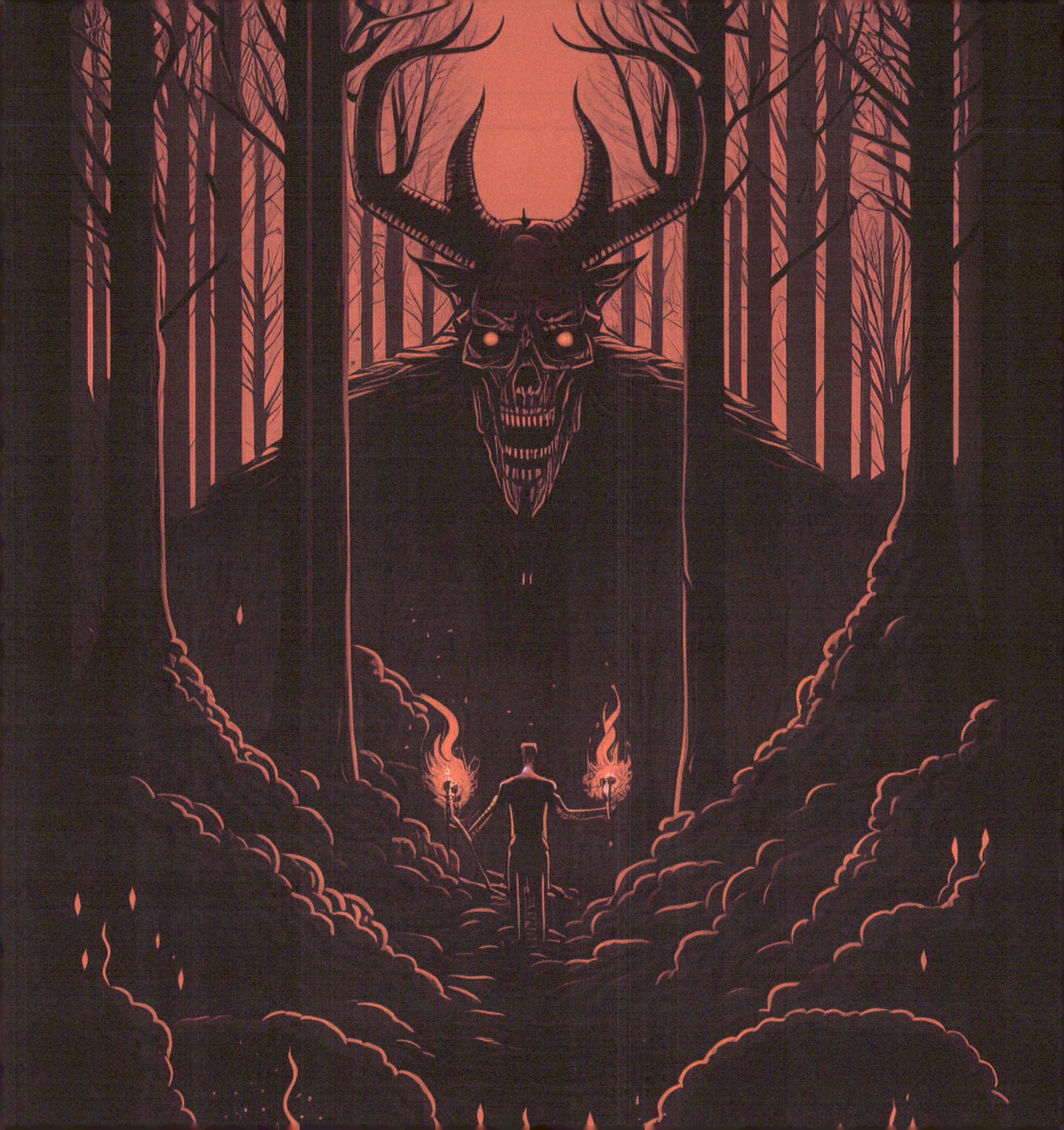

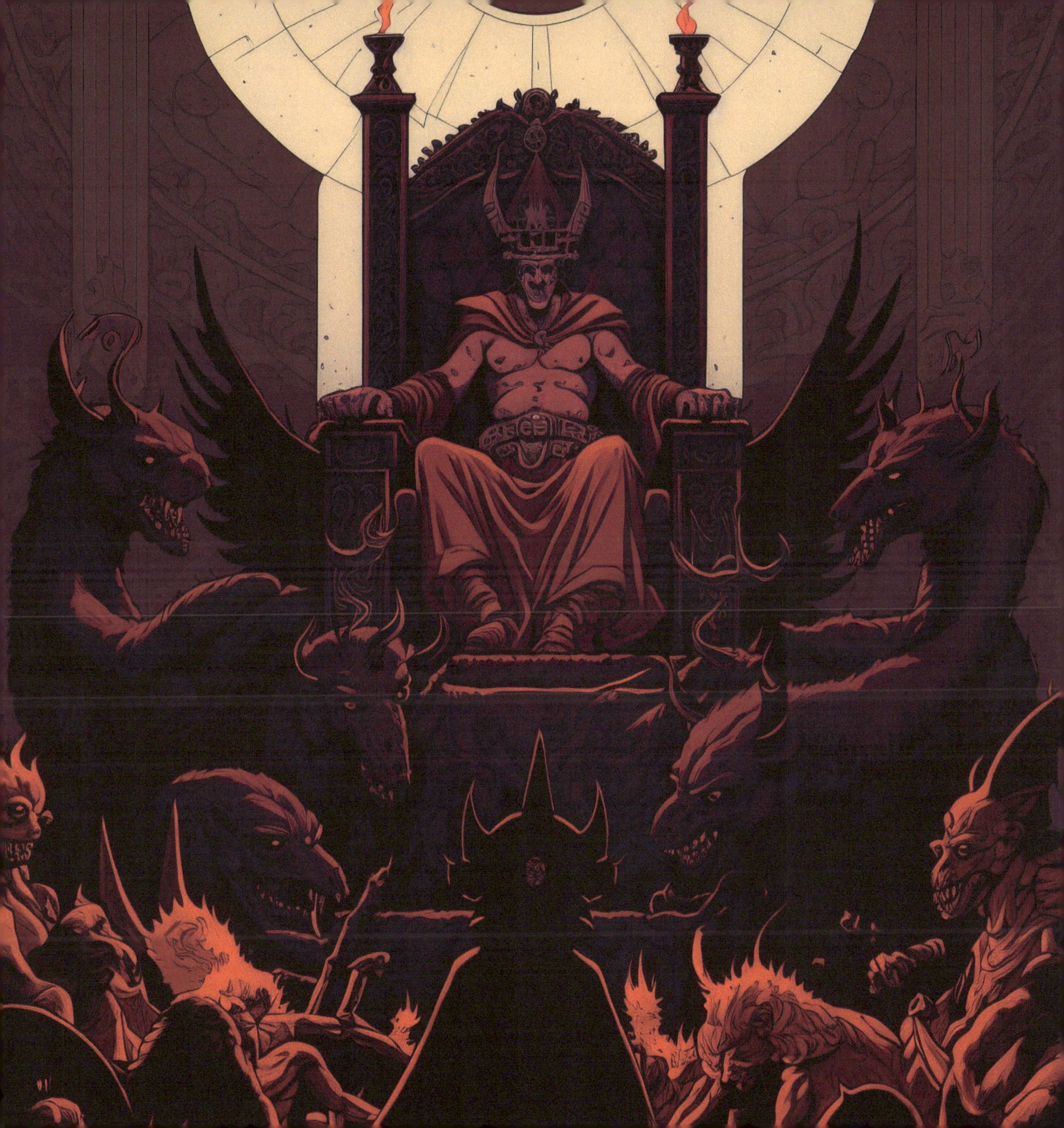

EPILOGUE

I wear a lot of shirts by the clothing brand "Blackcraft"
and because of that, some people assumed I was a satanist.
Which is pretty funny. The fact is, I don't really take stuff like that seriously.

But I think I ensured that I'd ignite next time I try to enter a church.
This book turned out to be pretty metal, and I'm not mad about it.

For now, this is supposed to be the final book in the "children's book" series.
I want to come up with new concepts and work on different stuff.
But who knows, when it comes to projects I constantly have new ideas.

I hope you enjoyed it.

Hail Satan, and see you in hell!
DANIEL